LOVE WHISPERS
IN SILENT STREETS

Nadakkavu, Kozhikode, Kerala, 673011
www.insightpublica.com
e-mail: insightpublica@gmail.com
Title: LOVE WHISPERS IN SILENT STREETS
Author: Mohammed Ali MundottuKandy
Pen Name : Mohammad Ali Poonur
Cover Design: Muhammed Nihal
First Edition: January 2025
All rights reserved.
Printed and Published by
InsightinPublica Printers & Publishers Pvt. Ltd.
ISBN - 978-93-5517-946-3

LOVE WHISPERS IN SILENT STREETS

SHORT STORIES

MOHAMMED ALI POONUR

INSIGHT PUBLICA®

66Life is a great tapestry. The individual is only an insig-
nifcant thread in an immense and miraculous pattern"

- Albert Einstein

Dedication

To my life partner, Noor Jahan, whose unwavering support and the fragrance of love and affection have always graced my journey.

Mohammed Ali Poonur, a seasoned marketing communication professional, holds a Master's degree and Associate credentials from CIM, UK, and IAA, New York. He has held managerial and directorial roles in various banks and corporations across the GCC. A passionate advocate for social service and education, he served twice as Chairman of the International Indian School, Riyadh—one of the largest schools in the world. He currently leads Chums Charity Malabar, an initiative dedicated to providing homes for the homeless.

An accomplished writer, Poonur has penned books and articles in both English and Malayalam. His works, which span political satire and fiction, have garnered critical acclaim.

Contact Information:
Heartland, Civil Station,
Calicut, Kerala, India 673020
WhatsApp: +971 562416362
Email: poonur@gmail.com

Sparks of Creativity

As a scribe of my own musings, I cannot claim the stature of a writer. Yet, the imageries imprinted on my subconscious through travels, events, relationships, and books have, at times, surfaced as narratives during rare and unpredictable moments. Are these stories biographical, reflections of reality, or driven by societal commitment? Truthfully, I don't know. What I do know is that I've endeavoured to do justice to the characters and their circumstances, weaving their experiences with authenticity and care.

Love Whispers in Silent Streets is a collection of 11 short stories, each exploring diverse and often unconventional themes. I am humbled to note that some of these subjects have rarely, if ever, been addressed by other writers.

For instance, "Kites of Hope" unfolds amidst the war-torn streets of Gaza, telling a poignant tale of young love overshadowed by conflict. "Love Whispers..." is inspired by a nurse's heart-wrenching social media voice clip during the COVID pandemic, lamenting the cruel neglect of the elderly due to scarce resources. "The Maiden Days" challenges the deeply ingrained superstition surrounding virginity and the hymen, a belief that persists even in modern societies. Meanwhile, "The Illumination" portrays a social worker's relentless fight against injustice, and "An Arabian Dream" takes readers on a young man's fantastical pursuit to find his father.

These stories are a blend of encounters, imagination, and the inspiration drawn from both. Each tale has its roots in the reality of life and the flights of creativity that transform it into fiction.

I hope these stories resonate with you as much as they did with me while bringing them to life.

Enjoy the journey.

Sincerely,

Mohammed Ali Poonur

CONTENTS

Kites Of Hope

"Y ou know, Abid, we Palestinians are like olive trees. Even if our roots are damaged or destroyed, we grow back stronger," Ayda wrote in her WhatsApp message. She had just completed her first prison sentence—for resisting Israeli settlers who attempted to destroy their drinking water source.

Abid had never met Ayda in person. Their connection began through her brother, his college classmate, and deepened over social media. It was her fierce blog posts against injustice and her leadership in the 'Intifada' that first drew him to her. But it was her wit, love for music and novels, and her unrelenting yearning for freedom that solidified their bond. Her solemn expressions, the dimple on her cheek, and her commanding yet graceful presence lingered in his mind, etched there unknowingly.

"You should visit Palestine next October, Abid, to truly see our occupied land, to feel its pulse and vibrancy," Ayda suggested. She and her friends had recently started a tourism initiative. More than a livelihood, it was a mission—to unveil the truth of the Palestinian struggle and expose the settlers' atrocities to the world.

October is the season when Palestine blooms. Rows of olive trees, heavy with light green fruits, create a sight that warms the heart. "You haven't written anything in a while," Ayda noted. "In that breathtaking landscape, poetry will find you—I'm sure of it."

Abid had been yearning for the olive groves—and for the girl who loved them. Ayda's subsequent messages brimmed with details about the tour program.

"We're creating an aura like no other, a chance to connect deeply with the heart of Palestine," she wrote. "You can join the farmers in harvesting olives—climbing the trees or picking fruits from the ground. Fill buckets and bags with the bounty of the land. Visitors will actively participate at every step. You'll also get to share a traditional lunch with the farmers. It will be an experience unlike anything you've ever had. And I'll be there with you, every step of the way."

Her enthusiasm leapt off the screen as she described the itinerary: a visit to Bethlehem, Hebron, Ramallah, the Arafat Museum, and the historic site of Prophet Saleh, famously tied to the 'Intifada'.

"Today, the olive harvest season, once a time of joy and security, serves as a poignant reminder of occupation—the land grabbing, the destruction of our fertile trees, and the overwhelming cruelty. But we resist this injustice every day. During the tour, you won't face challenges as a foreigner. The oppressors are careful about appearances for outsiders. It's an opportunity for us, too, to show the truth. Roads and military outposts, restricted to the occupiers, will be opened."

When Ayda spoke of olive trees, her passion was palpable. Her large eyes glowed, her words flowed with fervour. Olives, after all, are symbols of Palestinian identity.

"The olive tree can survive for thousands of years," she explained. "Some in our region are estimated to be over 2,000 years old and still bear fruit. You can't truly destroy an olive tree. Even if it's cut down or burned, it grows back, bearing fruit the very next spring. It's a miracle of resilience. This plant doesn't even need water to thrive. And the fruits it gives—considered sacred by all three Abrahamic religions—are a treasure trove of health and heritage."

"I don't think your tour company needs another PR officer," Abid teased.

Ayda's cheeks flushed, her dimples deepening as she laughed.

"I don't need to tell you that Palestine is a land steeped in history," she continued. "But it's also a place of stunning natural beauty—blue lakes shaped by nature and Bedouin villages where life is simple and pure. We're planning to end the trip with a desert camp. Imagine spending a night under an endless sky, its starry eyes watching over us. The tents, the stillness—it's magical. And October is perfect. The cool breeze from the Dead Sea, just as winter begins, adds an unforgettable charm."

"At night, visitors gather around the campfire to enjoy traditional Palestinian food, sip steaming Sulaimani tea, and listen to the adventurous tales of the Bedouins. The moon dances slowly between the hills until dawn.

As the sun rises behind the Jordan hills, casting its golden light over the Dead Sea and its surroundings, an almost sacred silence falls over everyone. In that moment, gratitude fills the air as they share these cherished experiences. Inevitably, someone whispers, "Is the rising sun always this beautiful?"

"Enough is enough. You've made me so excited—I'm in a hurry to get there. I can't wait for October," Abid declared.

"Me too," Ayda replied haltingly. "Just don't leave your vacation formalities to the eleventh hour."

What enticed Abid even more than the landscapes was the opportunity to truly know Ayda.

Abid busied himself preparing for the journey, gathering backpacks, clothes, shoes, food, and souvenirs for Ayda.

But October was still a month and a half away. Ayda's body language revealed her quiet anticipation, though, as always, she wouldn't openly express it.

Then, just days before his trip, everything changed.

A daring group of young Palestinians managed to outwit Israel's formidable intelligence and defence forces, launching an attack, taking hostages, and returning safely. It was a significant blow to Israel's pride and a turning point in the conflict.

Though saddened by the abrupt halt to Abid's travel plans, Ayda's words brimmed with pride.

"They want freedom from the horrors of the past," she wrote. "From being forced out of their homes at gunpoint, from polluted wells, from destroyed livelihoods, from the inability to move freely in their own land. They don't seek to be martyrs or heroes—they were dragged into this by relentless injustice. These un-rectifiable losses led to their bold actions. Let the war end, Abid. Then we can meet."

From that point, Ayda's messages became a "running commentary" on the war.

"Are you going to leave us, Mama?" a little girl asked, her tearful voice recounting her mother's last words before dying in a bombed-out home. "But I'll be alive in heaven, and I'll see you all." The child's words were laced with hope despite her unbearable loss.

A boy praised God for finding his kitten among the rubble. Stray cats, now orphaned like their owners, roamed the streets. Another child shared his scant food with them.

The resilience of the Palestinians was astounding. Bombed, orphaned, and stripped of basic human rights, they bore unimaginable agony. Yet, they blamed no one, clinging instead to a collective hope for a brighter tomorrow.

How brave these children were, how profound their words. They wrote their names on their hands with marker pens—Ayaan, Adnan, Farhan—beautiful names, to ensure their bodies could be identified if struck by a bomb. When the roar of a bomber sounded in the distance, they scattered, seeking an asylum that seemed nowhere nearer.

Ayda's voice cracked as she read aloud a viral poem by Zaina Assam. Overwhelmed, she couldn't finish.

"Write my name on my limbs, Mama

With an ink that won't wash away,

In your beautiful handwriting

On the arms of my brother and sister.

Write yours and Baba's names,

So when bombs destroy our homes and dreams,

The world will know we were one family…"

An elderly man sifted through piles of rubble in search of his granddaughter. After an hour, he found only the child's Barbie doll, still smiling. Death, delivered by a jet, had hidden the baby somewhere in the ruins. The old man raised his trembling hands to the sky, a silent plea to a world that seemed deaf to their suffering.

Stories like this were everywhere—children, dreams, and futures lost. Yet, amidst the devastation, the courage of a people enduring the unendurable shone through, their resilience unbroken, their hope steadfast.

A group of children sang the Palestinian national anthem, "Fedai." The lyrics were powerful and haunting.

Despite the threat of gunfire, health workers refused to abandon emergency patients, fully aware that their lives were at risk. They stood firm in the face of death, fulfilling their responsibilities. Many such heroes have sacrificed their lives selflessly.

We have nothing left to lose. Friends, loved ones, colleagues, doctors, teachers—everything is gone. Whether the war ends now or continues for years, the losses are irreversible. When will we return home? We don't know. We just don't know.

Often, we hear the faint cries of people trapped beneath the rubble of fallen buildings. But approaching to save them is impossible due to the threat of armed soldiers. The cries slowly fade into silence.

There are no beds or blankets to shield us from the cold nights. Clean drinking water has become a rare luxury. Contaminated water spreads disease, and pregnant women and children are especially vulnerable.

I know you've heard of these tragedies from the media, but I have no one to share my grief with, Abid. Everyone I held dear is gone. Still, I dream of the dove from Noah's Ark, carrying an olive branch to signal the end of the flood.

I've joined the United Nations Relief and Works Agency (UNRWA) as a volunteer, distributing food and supplies. It's a small way to fight starvation. Connectivity is challenging as we move from place to place, but I'll stay in touch as best I can.

Hunger is overwhelming. Food trucks sent by neighbouring countries are stuck at the border, awaiting military clearance. Recently, over a hundred people peacefully waiting for flour were shot dead by soldiers. These situations test our patience and our humanity, but losing control would be fatal.

The sight of thousands marching south with white flags, raised hands, and makeshift belongings, following Israel's orders, is both heartbreaking and unbearable. Even then, they are not safe from airstrikes and artillery.

For days, there were no more messages from Ayda. She was absent online, and the media brought only grim news. Abid couldn't sleep, eat, or focus. The thought of her in danger consumed him, testing the strength of their bond.

Finally, a message came, like a downpour after a drought.

"I know you must have been worried. I'm in a refugee camp now. The journey was harsh, and I had no internet access. I travelled in the trailer of a grain truck as fuel shortages have stopped most vehicles.

Here at the Rafah refugee camp, there are tents as far as the eye can see. I'm in charge of distributing food to hundreds of families. UN trucks rarely reach us because of intense inspections at the border, each taking hours. With no supplies to distribute, I have a lot of free time.

But hunger looms here, as dangerous as the bombs. I don't know how to console starving children in this freezing weather. I try to distract them by singing or teaching them basic lessons. Slowly, the children are adapting, though their eyes constantly drift toward the highway, hoping for the arrival of food trucks. If those massive lorries reach us, we'll have enough for a few days of relief."

Rafah's sky is now alive with kites in vibrant colours, most of them bearing the hues of the Palestinian flag. The children have found a way to escape the monotony of their harsh reality. Surrounded by kids clutching straw, yarn, and coloured paper, I've become an expert in crafting kites of all shapes and sizes.

Those patches of colour floating in Rafah's sky seem like tiny protests, trying to forget the brutal truths below. Beneath the kites lie cramped tents, where men and women scramble for water, food, and firewood. Yet amidst this chaos, the children's faces light up as their kites flicker in the sky—proof that even death, hunger, and freezing cold cannot crush their spirits.

Their joyous cries—shouting at the falling kites and cheering "hurrah" for the rising ones—bring a fleeting happiness to me, too. I whisper a prayer that the black smoke of bomber jets never darkens Rafah's sky again.

But the next day, grim news broke. Media outlets reported a war monger's prediction: the Rafah refugee camp could soon be targeted.

Abid immediately messaged Ayda, urging her to take every precaution. Yet unease gnawed at him. Friends and acquaintances he consulted advised against any rash decisions, warning him about the risks in such precarious times. But the thought of Ayda facing this unimaginable hardship alone left him restless and torn.

He paced the jogging track near his apartment, lost in thought. Amid his self-reflection, he resolved not to deceive his conscience. When someone you love is in danger, you need to be with them.

By the time Abid returned home, his decision was made. A newfound calm settled over him. He ate, packed his essentials, and prepared for the journey. With his passport and backpack in hand, he set out to reach his fiancée as soon as possible.

"Honey, I'm coming to Rafah. I'll wait for you at the Egyptian border," he wrote in a WhatsApp message to Ayda but hesitated to send it, fearing she might try to stop him.

Abid boarded the first available EgyptAir flight to Al Arish Airport, located about 45 kilometres from the Rafah border, driven by his determination to reach the one he loved.

Love Whispers in Silent Streets

"Stay at home; leaving home is punishable. We are in a war zone. People are only allowed to go out to buy medicine and in emergencies." The loudspeakers blared from civil security vehicles, and their echoes reverberated through the skyscrapers of the city of Milan. Esther quickened her pace, gripped by fear.

The once bustling streets, filled with vehicles, now appeared deserted. Only a few ambulances and army trucks with blaring sirens moved back and forth, carrying the weight of the dead. Despite the crematories on the city outskirts operating 24 hours a day, long queues had formed. Along the roads, soldiers in green and grey uniforms, armed with guns, stood in formation. Frequent checkpoints dotted the way, while pedestrians were a rare sight, prohibited from passing through. Esther, however, managed to proceed thanks to her ID card displaying the words 'Health Worker' in bold red letters. The policemen saluted and waved her on. She had to walk at least one and a half kilometres to reach her destination, as taxis and public transport were no longer available.

How swiftly everything had turned upside down. These streets used to be filled with music, as people of all ages danced in pubs, restaurants, and parks, celebrating love and jubilation. The lively atmosphere, accompanied by the vibrant glow of the city, had always been a unique experience for Esther. People would revel in the moment, echoing the sentiments of the Persian poet Omar Khayyam: "Enjoy this moment, for it is precious; do not think of tomorrow."

Today, the once cheerful faces wore a grim expression, and an air of solemnity hung over everything. Life had come to a standstill. Sickness and death cast a shadow over their previous happiness. The obituary columns in local newspapers could no longer fit within ten pages. Italian Prime Minister Giuseppe Conte acknowledged, "We no longer have separate red zones; now the entire Italy is a Zona Rosa." Sergi, an elderly man, remarked that he hadn't witnessed anything like this in Europe since World War II.

Esther wondered how Sergi was faring and prayed fervently for his well-being. Her thoughts were filled with horror when she considered Sergey, a septuagenarian knowing that a significant number of elderly individuals had succumbed to the coronavirus in Italy.

Her acquaintance with Sergi had been entirely coincidental. When she first arrived at Malpensa Airport in Milan, she felt anxious and worried. Customs had taken a long time to examine the dried fish pickles packed for her by her mother, Ammachi. The recruiting agency had promised that their representatives would be waiting outside the airport with a placard bearing her name. However, perhaps due to the late hour, there was no one to be seen. Clueless about making a phone call, Esther pushed her trolley to the end of the terminal. The exhausting eight-hour journey had left her feeling drained, and the realization that no one seemed to care about her well-being filled her with terror.

That's when she noticed an old man sitting in a corner, peering closely through a pair of black glasses, typing on his phone. Gathering her courage, she approached him and greeted him. He responded with a beautiful smile, which she found comforting— a momentary relief from her helplessness.

"Do you speak English?" she asked.

"Kena dee chi?" he replied in Italian, looking at her with a hint of curiosity, perhaps unsure about her accent. Determined to give it one more try, she paused and said, "Do... you... speak... English?"

"Of course, I do," the man replied, patting his chest. "An Oxford graduate. How can I help you, Miss?" Esther slowly and loudly presented her situation, showing him her hospital card.

"No need to speak so loudly," he touched his ear and gave a thumbs-up, indicating that his hearing was fine. Then he burst into laughter, and Esther joined in, finding his antics endearing. He introduced himself as Sergey and explained that he had come to pick up his grandson coming from Madrid but learned that the flight had been cancelled due to fog. "Anyway, it's fine. Your hospital nurses' accommodation is near where I live. We just need to share a cab. Don't worry; let's split the fare," he chuckled once more.

Upon reaching the hostel, he accompanied her inside. Sergey himself located the office of the chief warden. As he bid farewell, Esther took out fifty dollars to cover the taxi fare. "Oh, it's too much. I don't have any change, I'll get it from you later. I'm sure we we'll meet again." Esther hesitated, unsure of how to express her gratitude to the kind gentleman. He shook her hand, smiled, and departed.

The warden stowed her luggage in a locker, handed her the key, and gestured for her to follow. Although the lady remained silent, her smile conveyed a warmth that made Esther wonder if she was unable to speak or simply didn't know English.

"Welcome, Miss Esther Kuriakos. We were concerned when we didn't see you. We contacted the agent and the airport, wondering what happened." The tall, thin blonde woman motioned for Esther to take a seat and spoke in English with an Italian accent.

"I am Abrianna, the Chief Matron and Head of Nursing here," Abrianna introduced herself. Esther, unknowingly, floated a little in her chair. The other woman laughed and re-assured her, "Don't worry, I'm more of a friend than a boss. Don't you recognize me? I interviewed you on Skype." Due to the lack of light that day, her appearances were not very clear, but the voice friendly, asking professional questions, was familiar. "Esther can join us tomorrow. We'll have a week of induction and a hospital tour. You'll have an assistant with you," she said, and then rang the bell. A woman who appeared to be Filipina came and took Esther away.

In the induction class for new nurses, there were several foreigners, mostly Asians. After a brief welcome and intro-ductions by the HR manager, Abrianna took the lead. She emphasized the dignity of the nursing profession and the importance of providing services without any bias. "In Ita-ly, a significant portion of our population is elderly, so our patients will mostly be senior citizens. There will be times when your patience will be tested. You must maintain com-posure and always smile. This is the country where Flor-ence Nightingale was born. Let's not forget our tradition," Abrianna spoke passionately. Esther was amazed by Abri-anna's ability to describe things in such detail and with pro-fessionalism. It was then that Abrianna asked if Esther was familiar with the "Nurses Oath." Esther was taken aback by the sudden question but managed to recite it precisely and clearly because she had memorized it. Abrianna informed them that a slightly different Nightingale "Pledge" was in effect and handed out a copy of the pledge to everyone.

Next came the essential language learning and other as-pects of their new environment. Esther was amazed by the state-of-the-art facilities at the hospital and had read that Italy was at the forefront of emergency care. However, she didn't realize just how good it was until she experienced it firsthand. She was assigned to work as a nurse in the Pulmonology department, and it didn't take her long to adapt to the work since she had previous experience with the procedures. Esther's expertise and compassionate approach towards patients and colleagues quickly endeared her to everyone. The initial days were busy, with the need to grasp the workings of the latest bio machines and familiarize herself with the hospital's protocols. By the time she returned to the hostel after work, she would be exhausted, unable to even call her mother until the weekend. She thought about calling Sergey to thank him but couldn't find the time. A sense of guilt lingered in her mind.

One Saturday, when Esther arrived home from work, she found Sergey waiting for her in the guest room with a smile. She couldn't believe her eyes. She attempted to apologize, but only managed to utter a simple "sorry." Sergey responded kindly, understanding her busyness in a new job and environment. He genuinely inquired about her work and accommodation. His gestures and questions reminded her of her father, who used to visit her college hostel and worry about her food and facilities during her first year of nursing studies.

"It's the weekend, and the weather is excellent. Why don't we go for an outing? You should get to know the city of Milan," Sergey suggested. Esther stood there, momentarily unsure how to respond. "Hurry and freshen up if you agree with my suggestion. Don't worry, we'll be back before the hostel gate closes." A guided city tour was planned for the new staff from the hospital the next day, but Esther decided not to mention it to Sergey to avoid disappointing him. She reassured herself that there was nothing wrong with going out with a good man, as old as her father.

"I'll be right back," she said, walking into her room. After changing her clothes and obtaining permission from the warden, Esther joined Sergey who had arranged for a cab and was waiting for her. Outings with Sergey became more frequent on weekends. As she discovered his passion for Indian music and his extensive knowledge, she felt proud to have him as a friend. Sergey, a fan of Rafi Saab, would hum the singer's famous songs, and Esther would join in singing. They would then share a laugh. Against the backdrop of picturesque parks and tree-shaded walkways, those evenings became enchantingly beautiful.

One day, Abrianna called Esther to her office and inquired about Sergey. It seemed someone may have reported their friendship. "The hospital has certain rules and etiquette. The staff should have information about the people they are associated with. Italy is a land of mafias and such. It's for your safety," Abrianna explained apologetically. Esther was confident that Sergey could not be anything but a good man, although she felt a slight worry deep inside.

"Sergio Puotti, seventy-one year old former diplomat, who has goodness certificate from civil authority" Two days later, Abriana called on the phone. "The hospital has no objection to continuing the relationship. Sorry for bothering you, dear, it's just a formality." Although expected, this news brought immense joy to Esther.

Back home, the situation had started to improve. It had been a year and a half since Esther left for Italy. Her father had almost paid off the debts incurred for his children's education and other expenses using the savings Esther had transferred. "Now we have to renovate our house and find a suitable match for you. We receive many marriage proposals. Aren't there any good Christian guys out there? We would love to visit the Vatican after your wedding," her mother, Ammachi, shared her hopes and aspirations over the phone. Esther also wanted to fulfil their lifelong wish of visiting the Vatican and have them stay with her, even if just for a while. Unfortunately, her father's asthma and heart problems prevented the trip due to doctor's orders.

   Love Whispers In Silent Streerts

Weekend outings with Sergey continued, and with the addition of Esther's friends, the evenings became more vibrant. Singing, dancing, and storytelling provided a welcome escape from work-related stress for everyone, and Sergey's presence brought charm to the group. His songs, gestures during storytelling, and memorable jokes thrilled them all.

Suddenly, early one morning, Esther received a phone call from her mother's phone. It was her Uncle Papichettan on the other end. "Appachan (father)... it happened an hour and a half ago. Ammachi can't speak, she's overwhelmed."

Esther's tongue felt dry, and she sensed as if something was stuck in her throat. She lost her balance and fell off the bed. She couldn't comprehend what was happening to her. In a semi-conscious state, she felt as if her father was calling out to her. He had been a loving father who had sacrificed his life for the education and well-being of his children. Although she knew his illness was serious, she never imagined he would say goodbye so soon. Memories flashed before her eyes like scenes on a screen. She couldn't fulfil her father's dreams with her newfound prosperity. Destiny seemed like a paradox; she thought while sobbing. Tears streamed down her face.

Emma, her friend and colleague rushed across the room when she heard Esther's scream. She gently rubbed her forehead, wiping away her tears, and asked about the reason for her sorrow. Emma helped Esther lean on her and patted her head and chest, trying to calm her down.

Many colleagues offered their condolences in person, while others consoled Esther over the phone. The HR department suggested she take three days off from work to grieve, but Esther wanted to find solace by spending time with the patients. She regained her composure quickly. She called Ammachi and instructed her to arrange everything for the funeral service and other arrangements. "However, I can't bear it, daughter. Whenever your father regained consciousness, he kept asking for you..." Ammachi struggled to hold back her tears. She couldn't bear it any longer. After a brief silence, she hung up the phone.

"Sergey is asking for permission to take Esther to his house. If you want, you can go. It will be a good change in this situation," Abrianna suggested. Esther's friends packed her bag, and Sergey was waiting downstairs. "Take it easy, my darling girl," he said, kissing her forehead. Tears welled up in his eyes. Who was this man to her? An angel sent to comfort her in her time of need.

Arriving at the villa in Milan's affluent area, the front door swung open, revealing an elderly lady in a wheelchair. It was Mirabella, Sergey's wife. Esther had seen her photograph before. In Italian, she asked as they approached slowly, "Is this not Sergey's darling babe, now mine as well." Sergey helped her stand up, and she held Esther close with her frail hands.

Guiding the automatic wheelchair, Mirabella led Esther into the hall and said, "We cannot overcome fate. We can only accept it and find peace of mind." It felt as though Sergey, his wife, and grandchildren had planned various events to lift Esther's spirits and change her mindset. The children celebrated her presence by playing with her, giving her sauna baths, pretending to push her into the swimming pool, and singing and dancing together. Sergey played his music system, filling the air with melodious tunes.

Every now and then, Esther found herself reminiscing about her father. Addressing Sergey and the children, Mirabella said, "Leave Esther alone for a while. She needs time to reflect and heal from her loss." Although Esther had almost regained her composure, genuine laughter remained elusive. Four days passed swiftly, with those days added to her allowed leave and the weekend. Her fellow nurses must have taken over her workload and likely grew exhausted in the process. Duty awaited her the following day, so she hurriedly prepared to leave. Returning to the hostel, Esther realized she had a loving family in Italy, whom she could share her love with, just like her parents.

The hospital had been buzzed with activity, filled with patients suffering from seasonal ailments and more. A summer and winter went by, during which Esther had been promoted to the position of senior nurse, right below Abrianna. Esther had also started processing the visa papers to bring Ammachi to Italy. She believed that Ammachi would find solace in seeing the Pope and praying for her father.

Although news of a deadly virus originating from China had reached Italy, no one at the hospital took it seriously. Within a few days, the influx of patients began. The hospital beds quickly filled up, leaving no room for more patients. Desperate people struggled to breathe, and the availability of oxygen became inadequate. The scarcity of ventilators exacerbated the situation. Doctors and nurses worked tirelessly but felt helpless. Unfortunately, nearly half of the patients admitted to the hospital succumbed to the disease, with the majority being elderly. The medical director's voice echoed through the halls, "We cannot accept this situation. We need an exclusive hospital dedicated to Covid patients." His moustache and hands trembled as he spoke.

The following day, Esther and her colleagues received a notification that a Covid hospital had been established in Bersica, repurposing a military hospital. All nurses and doctors were required to relocate there. Fortunately, Bersica was not far from Milan.

Esther suppressed her rising fear, knowing that it was her responsibility to go. She resolved to face everything with courage. She called her mother to inform her about the situation. Ammachi, already aware of the events unfolding in Italy through the media, asked, "Can't you stay back and take on other responsibilities, Esther?"

"That would mean resigning from my job. Is it humane to turn back at this time of crisis?" Esther silently pondered. "Pray for me, mother. Everything will be okay."

Sergey needed to be informed as well. Although she started dialling his number, Esther felt the need to meet him in person and bid farewell. That's how this adventure had begun—an endless journey with an uncertain destination. Her feet ached, and exhaustion weighed heavily upon her. As she reached the next junction, relief washed over her. She recognized Sergey's mansion as the second one on the right.

Sergey tended to his beautiful garden, his eyes widening in surprise as he saw Esther approaching. "Comistai signore?" she greeted Sergey in Italian, asking how he was.

"Stobene, ragatza brillante. Comistai?" he replied, inquiring about her well-being.

"Angio Stöbene," she responded, assuring him of her own good health.

They discussed the situation in detail, and Sergey's immediate response was, "Can't you reconsider and not go?" However, everything had been said and understood. "Be very careful, wear masks and gloves, wash your hands with soap, and use sanitizer," she cautioned. Esther bade farewell to Sergey, Mirabella, and the grandchildren. Suddenly, she remembered the time when her father and mother had come to the airport to see her off. She discreetly wiped away her tears with a handkerchief. "Call me when you're free, and take care," Sergey waved goodbye. Esther nodded in acknowledgment. He arranged for a motorbike taxi to take her back, enabling her to reach the hostel without encountering any checkpoints along the way.

A huge military coach came to take them away in the morning. The entire nursing department was there, including Abriana; and doctors and other paramedics. Maybe because there was no traffic, they reached Bersica in less time. The coach stopped in front of a military barrack. That was their accommodation. A sergeant announced over the mike that all should report to the hospital within an hour. It was a command. Everything sounded an emergency.

".........This meeting is not to teach you how to treat patients. We know that Lombardy, which we were proud to have the best emergency service system in Europe, has become the epicentre of the corona virus. We were completely unprepared for this epidemic," a military doctor is speaking. The stars and insignia sewn into his uniform denoted his high rank.

"We have overtaken China in terms of death and morbidity. When we had fewer patients, we used to treat them luxuriously. But now we are unable to provide ICU facilities for patients who are struggling to breathe because of the excess of patients. We do not have enough ventilators. If there is an increase in patients, we will not have enough beds. This is where you have to show your efficiency. As economists say, optimal utilization of scarce equipment is the best option. This means that ventilators, ICUs, etc. should only be given to patients who are likely to be cured. Age range and general health of the patient can be used as criteria. Where relatively healthy people need treatment for a short time, the elderly and infirm may take longer or be ineffective. This may sound cruel. Let all of you reckon that this' the only way to save the nation from this scourge. Another important thing is to not forget to follow all the protocols while interacting with the people affected by Covid. You are the frontline warriors in the war. Nothing should happen to you. We have to win this war at any cost" He paused.

Esther left the meeting with a heavy heart. She remembered that although her nursing career was short, she had done nothing unfair in her memory. Denying treatment to the elderly, leaving them to die because of lack of equipment and facilities, was unacceptable to her. She started the work at the new facility disinterested. Esther prayed ardently that she would not cause injustice to anyone.

She found herself assigned to the first-floor ward, where relatively young and nonserious Covid patients were treated. Perhaps her skill in operating the medical equipment played a role in this decision. "Good luck," she whispered to herself, relieved that she wouldn't have to witness the heart-wrenching scenes of people gasping for breath and succumbing to the disease. However, a lingering hesitation crept within her. Wasn't this an escape from the harsh reality unfolding around her?

Days were passing by, with Italy ranking first in disease spread and deaths. The relentless cycle seemed destined to continue until a vaccine was discovered. Tragically, Esther knew many individuals who had succumbed to the disease, including brave health workers. Despite the limited resources at her disposal, Esther tirelessly worked to save the sick. The patients received treatment in the form of oxygen, administered in calculated increments and decrements, along with sedatives. However, there were no specific medicines available for the affliction. Though some reports suggested that a combination of hydroxychloroquine and azithromycin showed promise, certainty remained elusive.

From the far end of the ward, separated by a glass wall, a disheartening sight awaited onlookers. Dead bodies, meticulously arranged as per Covid protocol, were being transported on a steady conveyor belt from the mortuary to the ambulance parking lot. In those rare moments of respite, Esther would gaze upon this solemn procession, offering silent prayers for the departed souls.

One fateful day, when she arrived for her duty, Esther discovered that her schedule and ward assignment had been changed in the duty rotation. Now stationed on the third floor, she was tasked with caring for the most critical and elderly patients. Surprisingly, she felt an unexpected numbness overpowering any fear that might have arisen within her.

Esther commenced her rounds alongside the junior medical staff, moving through the ward where additional patients in critical condition awaited her care. The air was thick with desperation as many struggled to breathe, their laboured gasps permeating the room. As Esther progressed, she felt her heart race upon spotting a familiar face, struggling for every breath. Drawing closer, she was shocked to see that it was Sergey, her dear Sergey. With a mix of disbelief and concern, she examined the case sheet that confirmed his identity: Sergio Puotti, suffering from severe pneumonia and respiratory arrest.

"Signore," she called out to him, her voice filled with urgency. Sergio was in a semiconscious state, critically deprived of breath. Esther realized that a ventilator might be his only chance of survival. The nurse within her awakened, driven by a sense of purpose. She knew that a ventilator, previously used by a patient who had recovered, was available on the first floor. Its location was etched in her memory. Without hesitation, Esther sprinted past, paying no attention to her surroundings. The elevator was out of order, but Esther didn't wait; she swiftly descended the stairs.

Breathless, Esther reached the first floor and quickly informed Abrianna, who was in charge of the floor, of the situation. She swiftly manuvered the ventilator machine, and rushed towards the emergency lift. Abrianna called out to her, hastening to catch up. Together, they managed to connect the ventilator to Sergio's bedside, their actions fuelled by a combination of skill and desperation. A slight movement appeared on the monitor, and Esther fixated her gaze upon it, her prayers intertwined with her every breath.

The monitor initially displayed turmoil but gradually stabilized. Sergio's eyes fluttered open, and his lips moved as if attempting to speak. A tear rolled down Esther's cheek, a mix of relief and overwhelming emotions flooding her being. Moments of elation swirled around her, and she tightly gripped Abrianna's hand.

However, the monitor's stability wavered suddenly, and Esther's excitement turned to apprehension. In an instant, the curve on the monitor flattened, and a profound stillness filled the room. "Signore, I wasn't fortunate enough to find you sooner," Esther uttered through tearful sobs, overcome by a profound sense of loss. Her head throbbed, her body aching with exhaustion. Unable to withstand the waves of grief crashing against her heart, Esther swayed, on the verge of collapsing. In a tender act of support, Abrianna swiftly carried Esther to the adjacent bed, where she sought solace against the weight of her emotions, finding temporary respite in Sergey's presence.

The illumination

This is the tale of my hamlet nearly two decades ago. When I eloped from there, I didn't even have a distant thought of a coming back. Although a host of memories, lovable and otherwise, linger in my memory, I believe that the legend I'm going to narrate would go a long way to make you love or hate my village.

The subjugation by the tourism industry coupled with urbanization has considerably transformed the façade of the region, but it would be an exciting experience for any student of history to tread through the path of the ensued revolution.

As it is surrounded by steep hills and deep forest, the village could aptly be called a locked land. This might be the reason why it could stay an unsullied land for long without enticing invaders from far and near. In other words, 'Gaznies' and 'Ghories' were indifferent about this vast strip of terrain, for that matter

Residents were mostly migrant farmers who anchored in the village decades ago. Early birds enclosed the fertile and plain lands and established the right of ownership to themselves. Reminiscent of Australian and American migrations, here also history had been repeated. (Repetition is the destiny of history as always.) Aboriginals, the real sons of the soil, were cornered to the rocky and infertile south hills.

Majority of the farmers who migrated to the village were from lower strata of society and their situation was not too different from that of aboriginals. Primary amenities like toilets were not available to them or were ignorant about it.

In the early hours of the mornings, they went en-masse to the borders of the forest to attend to the call of nature. Here the ladies were given preference, an unwritten rule, to be broken most of the time. During the process of the excrement many of them were bitten by "thuvva", a bushy plant whose leaves cause itching, at the private parts. The affected, who couldn't stand the itching of (swollen) anuses, dived into the forest stream, cursing their destiny.

There were an elite class of people in the village, the descendants of early migrators who bounded the majority of the productive land for themselves. They were the superiors. Nick named as Adhikari, the village officer and his assistant also called 'kolkkaran' (land surveyor) were the only government officials who frequently crossed the forest and visited the village. Staying at the luxurious dwellings of Avaraachan and Pockeraaji, they clandestinely legalized the ownership of the land to a select few. The officials were amply remunerated with sumptuous night parties and monies in abundance.

The village could be seen as a replica of the whole of India – consisting of people who led a luxurious life, the middle class and the underprivileged masses, deep in debt due to excessive interest rates, ailments and other misfortunes, who were destined to be laborers permanently.

No sooner than the Muaddin, Kalanthan Mollaakka*, calls for the dusk prayer, a fearful silence envelops the village. After the prayer he closes the little mosque and strolls feebly his way through in the hazy light of a lantern to his hut in the valley. The village path then becomes deserted of humans. Dogs, jackals and big cats sway the narrow trail, howling and screaming, setting an air of fright.

Mollakka*, Velichappadu* (oracle) and some other parasitic individuals tactfully engineer the terrible atmosphere.

'Hey buddies, did you know I have had an encounter last night with a monster as tall as a palm tree carrying a flame in his long skeleton hand. He was crossing the pathway to the hilly forest. On his stomp he stared at me with his red bulging eyes. I was about to faint, but could catch hold of the talisman worn on my hips and recite 'zikrs*' I could remember. If anyone of you were in such a situation, you would have fallen scared and breathed your last instantly. It is better that all of you take care while going out after dusk.'

Velichappadu also would have his analogous 'tippani' for the other priest's words "Do not attempt to go near the ditch-poked path in the night. After sun set, evil spirits roam the way and many people had seen obnoxious single-breasted women and one-eyed men with demon looks. Always recite gods' names, protect yourselves and make sure that you and family stay put"

All these utterances take place at Kunhikkannan's fully-packed teashop when the laborers and their supervisors gather for their breakfast at ten in the morning. Although known as a teashop it's a market place in the village with a snack bar, restaurant and grocery all combined. Kunchikkannan also trades in agricultural products, he buys them from the farmers and send it to nearby towns by bullock-carts for sale. He only takes a little margin from the profits and rest is given to the farmers. Hence the ordinary people like him and give due respect to him.

On hearing Mollacka's and Velichappadu's stories, Kunchikkannan would chuckle and laugh in a repudiating style. One might feel as if there were a lot of mysteries behind his gestures and he seemed hiding a Pandora's Box of secrecies.

If you ask, he would say "Are you foolish enough to swallow all those cooked-up tales? All these are done in return for payment" For whom? To whom? There is no space for such queries. It may help enhance our curiosity, none else.

A paraplegic with a debilitated limb, due to polio infection, Kunchikkannan was healthy otherwise, with a six pack body, handsome looks and a captivating smile. It's no wonder that all beauties in the village are his regular customers.

Some of the recurring sights and sounds had amazed even those who did not believe in ghosts. On certain nights, the faint sound of pebbles falling on the window panes of a few houses could be heard. Shadows would dance around the buildings, and whispers of bangles and muffled female voices would fill the air near the ditch-poked path as mentioned by the Velichappadu.

Even after hearing these anecdotes, the only response you would receive is a mocking laughter from Kunhikkannan. As you stand there, stunned, his words strike you: "Read it all together, don't let yourself get overwhelmed; the pebble throwing and such are an invitation." Meanwhile, the villagers were troubled by the increasing number of young people disappearing in the forest and the presence of battered mothers. They attributed it all to ghosts, leaving them too frightened to question the mysterious occurrences.

Firoz was another significant figure in the village, standing out among the middle-class youth. His father sent him to a college in the nearby town to ensure he didn't waste his time playing with other children. Upon earning a degree in Sociology, Firoz developed numerous ideas to uplift the village. He saw electricity as the highest priority and dreamt of providing his fellow villagers with nights free from fear.

"They are creating a "fear psychosis" with the help of superstitions to fulfil their own disgusting desires. Don't let this happen. First of all, we need electricity."

Firoz rallied his energetic friends, encouraging them to join him in their mission. Together, they organized signature collections and consent forms as they traversed the village. Almost everyone was on board, except for a few followers of the village chiefs who spread counterpropaganda, fabricating false tales of danger. Unfortunately, they managed to deceive some vulnerable individuals.

"What is this boy trying to achieve? Does he want to disturb our peace of mind?" objected those who benefited from the darkness. Dakshayani, also known as 'Oottys', voiced her concerns, joined by Thresyamma, Meenakshi, and Kaisummu, who intensely prayed to their gods for assistance.

There were also attempts to pressure Firoz through his father. Pokharaji reached out to Firoz's father, urging him to divert his son from his chosen path. "Uncle Pokker, I am confident that Firoz won't do anything wrong. I don't know what else to do," responded Firoz's father, Antruka, steadfastly supporting his son. This unwavering family support bolstered Firoz's determination.

The villagers were eager to break free from the chains of darkness and bask in the enchantment of light. However, numerous obstacles still lay ahead. At times, these challenges made Firoz anxious, but he remained undeterred. His dream of a fair and beautiful homeland fuelled his energy.

Every morning, Firoz embarked on his journey with a briefcase filled with files, heading towards the District Headquarters or the state capital. Sometimes, it would take him three or four days to return. Each step he took served a sacred purpose, as Firoz refused to give up.

"Sahib, how are things progressing? When will we have electricity?" affectionately called Sahib by some due to his refined appearance, Firoz responded to Kumaran, who was ploughing the fields.

"Don't worry, Kumaran uncle. Everything is falling into place," Firoz assured him, and the unwavering faith of everyone in his abilities reinforced his determination.

As Firoz bid Kumaran farewell, Chirutha appeared before him, balancing a bundle of green grass on her head. A dimple appeared on her cheeks as she smiled, revealing a row of teeth.

"When will we have electricity, Sir?" Chirutha, who took the lead in wiring for her colony, inquired.

"It won't be long, sweetie," Firoz replied playfully. "I know you believe in me, and I won't let you down." Chirutha nodded, scratched her back with a scythe, and made her way towards the stream.

When he proceeded further ahead, Firoz spotted Suharabi, his fiancée, by the fence, pinching moringa leaves. As he approached, she must have quickly made an excuse upon seeing him. The beauty of the rays of the morning sun had made her even more captivating. Firoz, however, pretended not to notice and walked away.

"Firoz*..." came a desperate call from behind.

"Ah, who is this, my sweetheart?" Firoz turned around. Their marriage had been arranged, and were waiting for her exams to finish.

"Don't act like that, Firoz. If so, I know what to do,"

"Don't make it an issue, darling. You know my situation." Firoz replied.

They conversed for a while, and then Firoz left. As he bade farewell to her, he felt a newfound energy surging through him. Instinctively, he found himself humming a love song.

Firoz hurriedly walked, dismissing any lingering thoughts. If he missed the nine o'clock bus to town, he would be left without any transportation, and the day's plans would be ruined.

One by one, obstacles began to emerge. Consent was required from all property owners and householders along the seven kilometer route. Surprisingly, it was accomplished with relative ease. Moving through the forest seemed like the next challenge, but since it was government owned, Firoz believed it would be straightforward. However, there were hurdles in the form of environmentalists and animal lovers. The forest department proved to be troublemakers as well. Nonetheless, Firoz managed to overcome these obstacles by influencing the forest minister.

Then, a notification arrived from the Electricity Department. They informed Firoz that no power poles could be installed that far without a deposit to cover the expenses. But where would he find the funds? Firoz felt as if someone was pressing him hard against a wall. Fortunately, the Scheduled Tribes colony located at the end of the forest provided a much-needed advantage. The concerned department intervened and facilitated the necessary arrangements.

Nevertheless, the lack of budget allocation remained a significant hurdle, as a substantial amount of money was required to complete the project. Only the Chief Minister had the power to assist in this matter.

That's when a piece of unexpected good news arrived, surprising Firoz like a bolt from the blue. It came from a friend who worked in the media, that the assembly election would soon be announced. Firoz confirmed the news with the Secretariat, realizing that this was a golden opportunity. If they didn't act quickly, things could spiral out of control. Without electricity reaching the village before the announcement, they would be left waiting indefinitely.

Firoz's media friend took the initiative to arrange a meeting with the Chief Minister, securing a brief fifteen-minute slot for Firoz to present his case. The minister attentively listened to Firoz and immediately made a couple of phone calls to the concerned officials.

"Don't worry, Firoz. Your village will be illuminated next week," assured the Chief Minister in a reassuring tone. Firoz couldn't believe his ears and expressed his heartfelt gratitude while struggling to hold back tears of joy.

As Firoz disembarked from the bus and reached the village road, he noticed a vehicle from the electricity department waiting for him. The Assistant Engineer asked him, "Has the wiring been done? The order is to complete it on a war footing." Surprisingly, this same individual who had previously looked down upon Firoz's efforts was now eager to know how he had achieved this feat. He even inquired, "Do you personally know the Chief Minister?" Firoz simply smiled, leaving the assistant engineer intrigued about his connection to the higher authorities and pondering the possibility of a promotion.

Everything proceeded swiftly. Houses were inspected, transformers were installed, and even street lights were set up. Firoz couldn't help but acknowledge that the Chief Minister had thoroughly reviewed his petition.

The historic day finally arrived, and the entire village was adorned with decorations. People were in a jubilant mood, celebrating the long-awaited arrival of electricity. Children excitedly followed the linemen, offering any assistance they could.

Firoz and his friends worked to raise awareness and prevent accidents. Beepathu and Lakshmikutty, both educated individuals married to the village residents from houses that already had electricity connections, took charge of women's affairs.

At exactly six o'clock, the district collector arrived. Dusk was settling in, and darkness began to spread due to the proximity of the forest. Upon his arrival, the collector handed over a note from the Chief Minister to Firoz, apologizing for his absence due to important engagements and urging Firoz to inform him of any issues.

Reading the note, Firoz felt as if he were being touched by a feather and enveloped in a shield of safety.

As the collector switched on the transformer, the village erupted with light and resounded with cheers and shouts. Sweets were distributed, and a tea party was held. Janu brought a special sweet drink called "payasam," while Kunjayisu contributed a dish of eggs. Deenamma's sweet nut balls were enjoyed by all. They danced, sang, shared stories, and revelled in their joy until dawn.

The happiness of these innocent people brought a smile to Firoz's face. He had many more plans in mind for them - toilets, schools, and transportation facilities.

They celebrated fearlessly day and night, indulging in their hearts' content. Gradually, the village began returning to normalcy, and a couple of uneventful days passed by.

Then, in the middle of the night, a dreadful explosion shook the entire village, plunging it into darkness. Fear spread among the villagers as mothers clutched their children together. Were the fairies and ghosts angry? None of these explanations seemed futile. The villagers exchanged fearful glances but hesitated to go out and investigate.

Firoz awoke from his slumber, grabbed a torch, and prepared to investigate the cause of the explosion.

"Let it be dawn. Let's wait and see. It's not wise to go now," advised Antruka, his father, stopping him in his tracks.

However, the villagers couldn't contain their curiosity and rushed towards the transformer upon hearing the crows' cries in the early morning hours. What they witnessed was a horrifying sight. There lay a man, covered in cuts and burns, with a branch from an oak tree beside him. Wires and shards of ceramic were scattered around, as if they had exploded. Upon closer examination, they recognized him as one of the stewards of Ilayath.

Confusion filled the air as the villagers exchanged bewildered glances. It appeared that out of sincere loyalty to his master, or perhaps due to sheer ignorance, the man had attempted to cut the electric wires, unintentionally causing the destructive incident.

Suddenly, Kunjikannan burst into uncontrollable laughter from his shop. His infectious smile seemed to erase all worries and mysteries in an instant. His laughter spread like wildfire, infecting everyone present in the village. The villagers couldn't help but join in, laughing so loudly that it seemed the sky itself was cracking with joy.

Mollakka: A Muslim Priest*
Vellichappadu: A Hindu Priest*
Zikr: Reciting Prayers*

Afsoon

"Hey Murad, where are you? Have you crossed the Pagman Tunnel?" Instead of a reply, a mixture of voices in Pashto and Dari came over the phone. "one kilo of onions, two kilo of potatoes and some tomatoes…." Gulshan felt anxious as expected. "Jee Huzoor" (yes master), Murad's voice was heard from afar "We encountered beggars on the way, desperate and starving. You will be rewarded by God" he said. Was he trying to teach about the people of the Hindu Kush mountains? They endure hardships without asking for help, even in their dying moments. If Murad had made such a comment in font of Afsoon, She would have slapped him. Her pride in her Hindu Kush heritage was unwavering.

Memories of Afsoon left Gulshan with mixed feelings. Even after three years of marriage, she remained a mystery to him. Like the Hindu Kush mountains, she was both beautiful and majestic, or perhaps like an AK47 rifle – a seemingly harmless toy, yet ready to unleash chaos at any moment. Both the weapon and the Hindu Kush have made their mark on the world, just like Afsoon. The thought of a world without her was unfathomable for Gulshan.

Contemplating Afsoon's potential reaction to his actions, Gulshan reassured himself that he would help her understand his motives. He had to move on quickly and strategically. Falling into the para military's grasp would mean the end of everything.

Gulshan hastened his pace, walking two kilometers to Jabbar Bhaiya's workshop. The Government insignia had been removed from his official vehicle, a modified Chevrolet, to avoid drawing attention. Bhaiya's services were expensive but efficient. If the new Government officials or their spies spotted the vehicle, they would seize it without hesitation. The surroundings were treacherous, and one could never anticipate what might arouse suspicion. Punishment was swift and merciless, often a bullet. Gulshan could not help but notice the wind causing his makeover beard and turban to flutter, fearing they might fly away. Such grooming had been done by the palace beautician, who had worked for the former President and his wife.

Anger toward the former head of the nation surged within Gulshan. He had looted the treasury like a cowardly mouse and fled without resistance. Many believed that it had been planned with the Americans beforehand. During Hamid Karzai's tenure, Gulshan was appointed as in-charge of palace warehouse. Now, with the current President gone, the orphaned palace was under new rulers' control. The secret underground vault offered some solace, a place where the new guards might not find him easily. He knew the escape routes well. The warehouse was stocked with food and various supplies. There was a time Gulshan had contemplated distributing these items to the needy, an idea inspired by Afsoon. However, if the new commanders discovered the plan, they would cut-off his connection to the outside world forever.

Hakeem Mia had advised and arranged for the transportation of goods in three or four trucks, justifying it as a reward for Gulshan's long and service to the people. "Even if you sell this much of goods, it wouldn't be enough for your gratuity. Consider making some money and relocating to Europe or the Gulf countries. In the current situation, life would be challenging for young people like you in this country". Hakeem Mia tried to persuade Gulshan who was hesitant to do so. The sexagenarian, his foster father and mentor, was the one who gave Gulshan the courage to hold on to Kabul for so long.

Hakeem Mia himself arranged experienced drivers for the KabulJalalabad Road and loaded the merchandise. He arranged Murad and his friends to the job, knowing that they would engage in such piferages. It was an adventurous journey, and income from these illicit businesses served as an incentive for them. It's better to turn a blind eye to their cunningness. The people of the Hindu Kush mountains used to eagerly await for trucks from Karachi and Kabul which brought goods across the Khyber Pass. They had a wide variety of offerings, ranging from sheepskins, furs, honey, miswaks, sticks of oud and sandalwood, ointments to herbs. In return, they mainly bartered for food and clothing, accepting only dollars if cash was involved.

The Kabul Jalalabad highway, stretching 160 kilometers, is renowned as the most dangerous road in the world. It is a treacherous road with a long tunnel alongside the Afghan river, allowing passage for only two vehicles. The road is bordered by a half-meter high wire, overlooking a deep ditch. Accidents are frequent in this place, earning it the infamous nickname 'Valley of Death', with vehicles plunging 600 feet. While 'dacoit' hijackings and kidnappings pose a threat, the biggest danger here is the unruly racing and law violations by Afghan drivers. Numerous taxis with worn-out tires and faulty brakes, as well as overloaded uphill trucks skipping backwards, hairpin bends and falling snow, contribute to the high accident rate.

The next morning – could potentially be his last morning in Kabul, Gulshan realized. The trucks must have covered a significant distance by now, so there was no need to worry anymore. It was time to bid farewell to Hakeem Mia. Gulshan's heartbeat quickened feeling as if the threads of his life were straining and breaking, sensing his throat tighten. Mia had arranged someone to drive his car "Don't go alone during these troubled times" Gulshan felt a shiver run through his body. Was he losing his sense of security forever?

"Mia, take care and do not try to oppose them. Stay put and mind your own business", Gulshan warned.

"I can't live without self-esteem. I will fight till the end", said the man, gripping the revolver in his belt. Hakeem Mia wouldn't bow down to anyone.

Tears welled up in the grand old man's eyes as he bade farewell saying, "Allah Hafiz". Gulshan couldn't bear to stay there any longer. He asked the driver to take the car and waved goodbye. Gul covered his face and wept.

Now, straight to Badi village of Afsoon, east of Panchsheer valley.

The car loaded with fuel, rushed towards destination. Since it was early, the highway wasn't crowded. "We're not in a hurry. Let's take it slow. Use the GPS, in case it starts snowing, we might get lost" Gulshan said while handing over the phone to the driver.

Farewell to Kabul, his beloved city that shaped him into who he was. After this bend there would be a hilly road. The highway was guarded by Hindu Kush mountain ranges.

Even in his subconsciousness, Afsoon haunted him. Despite having "Tajaki" roots in common, the two had little to share. Nevertheless, from the moment they met, an inseparable bond formed between them.

Their acquaintance, which began through Instagram, took a while to solidify. Afsoon's activities promoting women's empowerment and protecting orphaned children were met with suspicion by his family. Ammi (his mother) questioned "I wonder if Gul also supports her women's liberation ideals. Is she one of those so-called liberal city dwellers, flaunting their vanity and ideals?"

"Anyway, let's visit her home and village", she suggested. And so, they made their way to Afsoon's Badi village.

"She's an angel Gul. Like Florence Nightingale or Mother Theresa" After the visit Gulshan's mother marvelled at the girls Afsoon protected at the orphanage and the organic farm she managed. Afsoon would provide shelter for girls orphaned due to war and displacement, with state-of-the-art facilities, all funded by the income from organic farming.

"It's remarkable to see such a young girl doing all these. People like her deserve the Nobel Prize", she added.

Gulshan also had a philanthropic inclination, so supporting Afsoon was not a difficult decision. The only requirement Afsoon had was her service activities should not face any obstacle from Gulshan and that they would always stand for justice.

They celebrated their marriage with the residents of the orphanage. Gulshan suggested going to Europe or elsewhere for honeymoon, but wasn't possible due to foreign NGOs frequently visiting the orphanage.

Afsoon also questioned the need to leave such a beautiful place, asking "why go somewhere else when we have this paradise?" They spent alternating nights camping in the breathtaking valleys of the mountains. The children from Afsoon's institute sang and danced, making those evenings truly memorable. During this time, Gulshan also developed an interest in organic farming.

Over that time, an incident left Gulshan dumbfounded. As they wandered aimlessly, playing in the snow, an hour and half away from the visitors' balcony where they could experience the sensation of flying amidst the passing clouds, a foreign soldier commanded them to stop.

"Stop right there, both of you, and put your hands up"

the man in uniform approached swiftly. Pointing his gun, he declared, "Don't you know this is a restricted area? You'll be taken to Jail in Kabul, and the court will decide your punishment."

"No…..no. This is our country. What right do you have here?" Afsoon exclaimed defiantly. The soldier appeared surprised by her English accent.

"Listen, she's quite charming, so I'll make a deal. Let her spend half an hour with me in the cabin, and both of you can go free, without any charges", the soldier proposed, gesturing with his gun. Gulshan's anger boiled over. Before Afsoon could stop him, he punched the soldier with all his might. The man staggered and fell, but he quickly regained his composure, striking Gulshan with the butt of his gun and handcuffing him.

The soldier whispered to Afsoon, "Look lady, he can't do anything now. I have some dollars with me, I'll give them all to you. I'm just asking for a few minutes." He pointed the gun, and Afsoon winked at a restless Gulshan, signalling that she had a plan. The soldier opened his revolver holster to reveal the stash of currencies he had kept. Afsoon carefully bent down as if examining the money, but instead, she gently caressed his groin through his pants. The soldier, ecstatic from the intimate touch, reclined in pleasure. In a split second, with the skill of a trained athlete, Afsoon swiftly positioned herself between the soldier's legs and fired bullets from a hidden gun within her abaya, piercing his body. Blood sprayed in all directions like a mist. His lifeless body flew half a meter into the air before landing on the wire fence.

"Gul, let's get out of here immediately. His comrades might arrive at any moment," Afsoon urged, grabbing Gulshan and using her firearm to cut his handcuffs. "Where did you hide the gun?" Gulshan asked her. Afsoon simply laughed. "They assume that all women in the world are whores. I didn't intend to kill, but otherwise, he would have shot you and taken me captive." Fortuitously, strong winds and heavy snowfall suddenly enveloped them, making it impossible for anyone to find them. Nevertheless, they hastily departed, with Afsoon mostly carrying Gulshan along the way…….

"Sir, a call for you," Gulshan was startled as the driver shook him. They had parked the car in a crowded parking area, with a long line of vehicles stretching as far as the eye could see. It seemed that there might be an obstruction in the tunnel ahead.

"Jee Huzoor (yes boss)," came Murad's voice on the phone. "Sir, we have arrived at Badi. Ma'am doesn't allow carriages inside. She's standing at the gate, holding a gun."

Gulshan's mind raced, trying to understand Afsoon's intentions. How could he convince her otherwise? He pondered the situation with concern.

"Gul. It shouldn't be unloaded here. It belongs to the entire nation," Afsoon responded to Gulshan's call, unwilling to yield.

"Consider the circumstances, Afsoon. If we don't take it, someone else might misuse it. Alternatively, think of it as my retirement pension," Gulshan reasoned.

Gulshan's thoughts turned to Ilmat Yar, Afsoon's teacher and uncle. Perhaps he could help bring her to her senses. He swiftly dialled Ilmat Yar's number, hoping for guidance. However, to his surprise, Ilmat Yar saw nothing wrong with Afsoon's stance. It seemed the teacher and the disciple shared the same perspective.

"In any case, you brought it here. Let's divide it, giving half to the needy in the village and the other half to the orphanage," Ilmat suggested and Afsoon agreed. Gulshan found himself with no other choice but to agree with her decision……..

"Let us live here, Gul, using our strength to protect the destitute and cultivate organic farming. There's no need to seek livelihood in another country. And we'll work towards obtaining UNICEF approval as well," Afsoon expressed, affectionately caressing Gulshan's muscles.

Gulshan, lying lazily on her lap, appeared lost in his own thoughts, seemingly oblivious to her words.

"In these precious moments, I yearn to immerse myself in you and gaze into your enchanting eyes,……." he softly hummed a Pashto lyric, embracing Afsoon with passionate intensity.

The Maiden Days

As she climbed the stairs to Gynaecologist Sharmaji's second-floor clinic, the overwhelming scent of medicine and antiseptics made her head spin. Years had passed, yet there were hardly any noticeable changes. The steps were now adorned with marble and fitted with steel handrails. The waiting area had slightly expanded, providing additional seating. A stout middle-aged woman, the receptionist, glanced at her with confusion, her face contorted as she struggled to contain a mouthful of saliva from chewing Pan Masala. With a hint of unease, she entered the chilly room. Apologizing for her tardiness, she informed the receptionist that she had an appointment booked and was half an hour late. The receptionist replied indifferently,

"No worries, there might be a slight delay. Dada (a gang leader) in this neighbourhood has an emergency case. The doctor will attend to other patients only after that."

The place was crowded with patients, mostly young women accompanied by their mothers. A few came with their husbands or partners. Fear and embarrassment were evident on everyone's faces. Most of them were likely victims of desperate circumstances—those who had been deceived by false promises, those who had fallen prey to criminal gangs, and those facing financial constraints that made it impossible to support an additional family member. Her attention was drawn to the notice board in the room. It displayed exorbitant rates for various procedures: abortion starting from six months and below, virginity tests, hymen repair... all commanding hefty sums. Strangely, there were no rates mentioned for pregnancy care or delivery, even though the doctor was an obstetrician. It was clear that the doctor was profiting from exploiting people's self-respect and fears.

Beside her, a slender woman with wheat-coloured skin leaned her head on a man's shoulder, whimpering softly. He comforted her by gently rubbing her back. It seemed that the abortion procedure was weighing heavily on her. When the whimpering escalated into sobs, he tenderly carried her outside.

Suddenly, a cry of pain echoed from within the clinic, gradually fading into a moan. After a while, a man dressed in traditional attire, wearing a silk kurta and adorned with gemstone rings, stormed into the clinic with three associates. The receptionist hurriedly stood up, folding her hands in respect. "That must be Dada from the neighbourhood," she thought. There were whispers and commotion inside the clinic.

Realizing it might be too late, she slowly drifted off to sleep.

She couldn't help but feel sorry for herself, being in this despicable and disheartening environment once again, even though she had been here three seasons before. It was all because of her father's beliefs. Her father, a loving but traditional man, insisted on following his customs and convictions. She wondered how certain African tribal customs had become deeply ingrained in him. Her mother, Amma, who had grown up in the rural environment of Kerala, held a liberal mindset and despised such practices. Govardhan Kotyal and Lakshmi Kutty had fallen in love and gotten married while working at a school in a mining town in the Congo.

Perhaps her mother had been drawn to Abba, as she called her father, due to his charisma and vitality, as there were no other similarities between them. He strongly believed in frequent virginity checks for girls.

Abba, born and raised in the Congo as the son of a miner, embraced local tribal customs with great enthusiasm. As soon as she reached puberty, she was taken to Sharmaji for examinations every three months. The physician's chubby fingers probed inside her, searching for any blemishes on her delicate skin. She squirmed in tingling pain while two nurses restrained her. These checks occurred whenever her male cousins visited or after a school excursion.

"Wardoo(Gowardhan), this is not how we should teach children about morality. We should educate them about resisting temptations through relatable examples and convince them of the dangers," her mother objected, knowing he wouldn't give in.

"Lachoo (Lakshmi), I know you Mallus are liberals. But let's not forget the community's practice of allowing upper-caste men for clandestine relations. Marriage is a gift of virginity. I want to present my unsullied Rukku to an eligible young man," Amma's pride seemed wounded. Was a confrontation about to unfold? But realizing it was futile, she backed off, as usual.

When Rukmini reached maturity, her strong opposition forced Abba to change his mind. In the meantime, a court order from Maharashtra banned virginity checks, preventing him from taking Rukmini for such examinations.

"Darling, don't be upset about your father's actions. Consider it a manifestation of deep-rooted superstitions," Amma tried to convince Rukmini when she was old enough to understand. "He loves us intensely, as much as life itself. The influence of his African past compels him to act this way. To illustrate, let me share an incident from our honeymoon. On the first morning, when he discovered the blood-stained bedsheet, he became ecstatic. It was evidence of my virginity before marriage. He danced around joyfully. The next day, he organized a party at the miners' club to announce and celebrate this. I felt ashamed, as if my skin was peeling off."

In Congo, this was a common practice at that time. Can we even fathom such customs in our own country?" Amma often expressed her thoughts openly. "Sometimes, I shudder at the thought that if we hadn't relocated from Congo to India when you were born, your father might have considered having you undergo circumcision, which was a normal practice there. Why blame the Africans alone? Even in societies we consider cultured, like the West, I've heard of extensive secretive tests conducted to ensure a bride's virginity before marriage. Despite the progress the world has made, there are still many men who view women merely as sexual objects." The seeds of revenge began to smoulder in her mind, fuelled by a strong desire to rid herself of the membrane that felt like an unwanted part of her body. Her attention was caught by a boy in her second language class who always seemed to cast seductive glances her way, accompanied by affectionate gestures from a distance. Rukmini assessed him carefully, noting his physical strength and attractiveness, but also his youthful appearance. She believed he could help her achieve her goal, but she didn't see a future with him. Rukmini encouraged his advances, and one afternoon, when his parents were out, they went to his house, where she fulfilled her desires.

As the broken skin stretched and flakes of tissue peeled away, she felt a mixture of sensations, but it wasn't an unforgettable experience for her. The boy, on the other hand, seemed to derive great pleasure from it and was left exhausted. In a rush, she got up and pushed him aside, noticing stains of blood on the bedsheets. When he expressed concern and showed worry about washing and drying the sheets before his mother returned, she couldn't help but laugh before swiftly leaving without offering any assistance.

Although she initially felt a sense of satisfaction from her act of revenge, Rukmini soon began to feel an emptiness within. As a woman, she couldn't shake the feeling that she had lost something precious in that moment, and she was consumed by regret. She questioned the purpose and value of everything she had done.

By the time she completed her graduation, Abba had signed up on multiple matrimonial sites, and discussions about potential grooms became a frequent topic of conversation at home. Factors such as caste, occupation, status, age, colour, and height were meticulously considered. Rukmini distanced herself from these discussions, claiming she had no specific preferences and leaving the decision to her parents. However, the discussions often revolved around matters of status and origin, leading to arguments between her parents. Regardless, Rukmini began to feel that it was time to embark on married life.

It was then that Abba introduced the idea of a suitable boy named Varun, who was smart, of Malayali descent, handsome, tall, and working as a junior manager in a company. Abba humorously added, "The only problem is his origin from Kerala." Laughter filled the room at the playful remark.

The mother and Rukmini found joy in the fact that the boy had Malayali roots, as it made it easier to inquire about his family in Kerala. Rukmini recognized Varun from a photo as the person who had delivered impressive presentations on marketing communications at the Executive Club. She briefly considered calling him to offer congratulations but dismissed the idea, fearing it could lead to the start of a relationship.

The marriage discussions progressed rapidly. Amma

took charge of investigations in the countryside, while Abba handled matters in Delhi. It took just a week for Rukmini and Varun to meet, and their families get acquainted. The wedding was scheduled to take place in a month.

"Rukku, I wasn't planning to marry so soon and was resisting my parents' pressure. But when I saw you, everything changed, and I had to adjust my plans. I was afraid that if I delayed our union any further, I might lose this beautiful darling," Varun confessed to Rukmini while they strolled through the Buddha Jayanti Park, holding each other closely and enjoying the beauty of winter flowers. Rukmini's cheeks flushed, and her eyes sparkled as she felt a surge of excitement. Sensing her change in expression, Varun brought her face close to his and asked, "What's wrong, darling? Did I do something to upset you?" She laughed and shook her head, replying, "No, nothing."

But deep down, Rukmini carried a lingering guilt that haunted her day and night. The fear of revealing her secret and the thought of being exposed as impure tormented her. How long could she keep this hidden? Would she be branded as deceitful if Varun ever found out? She hastily made an excuse of a headache and rushed home.

Aunt Maggie, whom she had always considered an older sister and confidante, shared her insights on society's deeply ingrained respect for the concept of virginity. "Most men insist that their future bride should be a virgin, regardless of their own dishonest and reckless lives. Do you want to waste your life dwelling on something that happened by mistake?" Maggie questioned her, when she sought guidance.

Aunt Maggie advised her to think more practically. She suggested that Rukmini invite Varun to a restaurant one day, explaining that she wanted to discuss something important. During their conversation, Rukmini should be honest and sincere, explaining that the incident was an inadvertent accident and that there were no emotional attachments with the boy involved. If Varun was open-minded, he might accept Rukmini and trust in her innocence. If not, she would lose him forever.

Rukmini tightly gripped Maggie's hand, tears welling up in her eyes. "Aunt, I can't take that risk. I want him," she said amidst sobs.

"That's where technology comes in. I don't know if you've heard in the news, but a nun in Kerala who was accused of sexual relations had her 'holy skin' surgically reconstructed to prove her virginity. It's not a miracle; it's happening all over the world every day,"

"Unfortunately, this belief is based on mere myth, one that has existed for centuries, even in civilized societies. Scientifically speaking, the presence or absence of the hymen is not proof of a woman's virginity. The hymen can be broken through sports or other physical exertion. Sometimes, even after intercourse, the hymen remains intact," Aunt Maggie explained, though Rukmini wasn't particularly interested in the scientific explanation.

Rukmini had made up her mind. In order to restore her virginity surgically and provide Varun with a natural experience, she disregarded suggestions of using pills to simulate the right sensations.

During her investigation, Rukmini discovered that some abortion clinics in South Delhi were also performing hymenoplasty. This led her to the same clinic where her father had previously brought her for virginity checks.

"Rukmini Kotyal," the nurse called, startling her. The waiting room was mostly empty. "I called you twice. Where have you been?" Rukmini gave the nurse a soft smile, lazily checked her watch, and walked into the doctor's room.

"Please come in, my Kotyal's daughter," Dr. Sharma greeted her. His face and eyes reminded her of an owl, and

Rukmini couldn't help but feel a wave of disgust as she noticed his fat fingers, which had invaded her during the virginity check, moving as if typing on a keyboard. She struggled to control the nausea that washed over her.

"How's your dad doing?"

"Abba is on an official tour."

"What can I do for you, darling girl?" the doctor asked, gently touching her abdomen. "How many months?" His obscene giggle filled the room, further repulsing Rukmini. She shared the purpose of her visit, and he burst into laughter upon hearing the matter.

"Don't worry. It will only take half an hour."

"Please take extra care; she is my friend Kotyal's daughter," he said to the nurse who came to escort Rukmini away in a wheelchair.

As she lay in the operating theatre, the doctor entered wearing a mask, gloves, and a surgical gown. Rukmini felt lucky that she wouldn't have to see the owl-like face throughout the procedure.

"There won't be much pain. But it is our duty to ask: Is local anaesthesia sufficient, or should we go for general anaesthesia?"

Rukmini opted for general anaesthesia, hoping to escape the vile surroundings and forget everything for a while.

"It might be a bit expensive."

"No problem." All she remembered was a triangular-shaped object being placed between her thighs. Then she felt as if she was being carried away to a different world by Varun, floating together, absorbed in the marvellous sights of a colourful locale... Varun would disappear from time to time, and she would call out to him...

"Are you okay? Everything is over now. If you don't feel tired, you may go," the nurse said as she woke Rukmini up.

Aside from a slight stretching sensation at the bottom, Rukmini was in good spirits. Antibiotics and creams were prescribed. "Be careful for two weeks. Avoid strenuous work. Don't use tampons," the nurse advised, handing her the bill. A small discount was given on her father's account. After transferring the money via Google Pay, Rukmini thanked and bid farewell to Dr. Sharma. "Okay, daughter. Now you are absolutely fresh. Call me if you have any doubts. And don't forget to invite me to the wedding," the doctor smiled and waved at her.

A week passed with internal discomfort, thickening, and bleeding. Rukmini recovered faster than she had expected. She felt smarter and more confident. The wedding day was approaching, and Varun called her daily. However, she avoided meeting him, citing a cold and fever.

"I need to see you today," Varun's voice came through the telephone on a Sunday morning. "Would you please meet me at the coffee house in the evening?" He ended the call without providing any further explanation.

Fear gripped Rukmini as she wondered about the reason behind Varun's sudden demand for a meeting. Did he discover something about her past actions? Her heart raced, and she hurriedly entered the eatery in search of Varun. There he sat, in a cozy corner, wearing his captivating smile. Dressed in a beige-coloured kurta, he looked even more handsome. He reached out and grabbed Rukmini's hand, holding her close.

"Why, Varun, are you in such a hurry?" she asked, trying to lighten the mood.

"I always want to see you," he replied, and Rukmini breathed a sigh of relief. "But our video calls can't compare to being physically present." He continued caressing her hand. "Besides, we have a lot to discuss before the function."

"Do you have any plans in mind for the honeymoon?" Rukmini inquired.

"We can celebrate it in a hill station or a similar place. I leave the choice to you," he replied.

The wedding celebrations blended Malayali and Kothi customs. There were dances and songs, but the "Nadswara Mela" and "Thayambaka" (musical) performances were particularly entertaining for the guests.

When the program concluded, a decorated limousine arrived at the wedding hall's entrance, ready to take the newlyweds to Shimla. All these arrangements were part of Abba's efforts to make the event truly memorable.

Rukmini felt a deep sense of remorse for not appreciating her father's affection and misjudging his intentions. Overwhelmed by emotion, she impulsively leaned on Abba's shoulder and sobbed uncontrollably. Bidding farewell to her mother and parents in-law, she touched their feet before leaving.

During their journey, the villages of Punjab and Haryana basked in the warm glow of the evening sun, while the sunset over the hills of Himachal added a touch of magic to the trip. They arrived at the hotel late at night. The moonlit pine trees and snow- covered hills created an ethereal atmosphere, as if nature itself was conspiring to foster love. As Varun went to the reception for check-in, she ambled along the compound's footpath, lost in a dreamlike state.

"Rukku, where were you? I was worried sick not seeing you," Varun came rushing towards her, concerned. He gently kissed her, pulled her close, and guided her back to the hotel. "Varun, let's take a walk in the open air for a while," she suggested.

"Not tonight, it's late. We have plenty of time in the days ahead," Varun replied.

Upon entering their hotel suite, Varun picked up the

menu and asked her to order food. "There's a good restaurant on this floor," she informed him.

"Honey, let's not waste time. We can savour these precious moments to the fullest," he urged. She hurriedly placed the food order and retreated to the bathroom. When she emerged in her bathrobe, the food had already been delivered. Varun, dressed in pyjamas, awaited her. She quickly changed into her night dress.

As they sat down for dinner, Varun spoke, "Rukku, we're embarking on a new life together. Let's open our hearts and discuss our hopes, aspirations, and even our past relationships." He continued, "I'll share details about my previous encounters, and I encourage you to do the same."

In that moment, Aunt Maggie's advice echoed in her mind, warning her to be cautious about revealing her past relationships. "My life hasn't been particularly eventful in that regard. I've had some close female friends, but nothing more," Rukmini replied cautiously.

"Are you a lesbian?" Varun inquired abruptly.

"No, I've never had any physical relations with anyone. Self-indulgence has been rare," she responded, feeling her heart race. She took a sip of water to mask any change in her facial expression.

"You seem like a simple girl from the countryside, whereas I'm the complete opposite," Varun began, delving into his own sexual adventures. From encounters with the housemaid to classmates, teachers, and colleagues... Rukmini covered her ears, unable to bear the details.

Is this the culmination I was so worried about? she scornfully thought.

"But all of that is in the past. It's just you and me now. Honestly, I don't deserve someone as pure as you," Varun admitted, attempting to reassure her. Whispering to each other, they nestled under the comforter. She was slowly discovering the exquisite pleasure of the man's intimacy. Time seemed suspended within her, like a delightful tingle, even as the hours slipped by. Upon waking in the early morning hours, she savoured the events of the night as a sweet dream. Her body tingled with a pleasant ache. She jokingly likened herself to a paddy field after a bull race. Despite the bloodstains on the bedspread, she decided not to show it to Varun, assuming he wouldn't find it noteworthy. He lay in a deep slumber, holding onto her tightly.

Carefully extricating herself from his embrace, she rose from the bed. Humming a love song, she brewed coffee using the machine and retreated to the expansive balcony. The panoramic view of snow-capped mountains and a cloudy sky intertwined, creating a mesmerizing sight. The vibrant blend of colours uplifted her spirits.

However, self-loathing seeped in as she recalled the days leading up to their wedding - her stubbornness, the futile attempts to regain her virginity, and the lies she had told Varun. Thoughts of his mysterious and questionable relationships tormented her, leaving her despondent, wondering if she would forever remain just one of his many girlfriends. Coldness and fear took hold, compelling her to retreat back to the room. She snuggled into the comforter, seeking solace in the warmth of Varun's chest.

An Arabian Dream

"How about a blanket, sir?" As Majid emerged from his slumber, he found himself face-to-face with an enchanting, blue-eyed girl. The air hostess appeared to be Armenian, her presence a welcome sight. Leaning down with care, she gently covered Majid with a blanket.

The early morning departure had left him exhausted, the rush of completing all the necessary formalities taking its toll. "So nice of you," he murmured appreciatively, as she opened the tray table and put the menu on it. The hostess took out a pad and pencil from her pocket, ready to take his order.

"Whenever you're ready, sir," she whispered softly before stepping away, noticing his impending drift back into sleep.

Just then, the captain's voice resonated through the sound system, affirming his unwavering competence. He provided details about the flight's altitude and the need for a detour due to ongoing conflict in Yemen, but assured the passengers that punctuality would still be attempted. Majid bid farewell to sleep as he listened to the captain's announcement.

It was Majid's second visit to the Gulf, and most of his fellow passengers were either working or seeking employment in the region. The Arabian subcontinent remained a safe haven even after three decades—a comforting thought.

With a playful recollection, he thought to himself that despite holding a work visa, he was not there for sustenance but rather to search for his roots.

Joffrey, the company's vice president, expressed great joy upon hearing Majid's decision to come. His elation resonated through the phone as he whistled a special melody. "I need you, man, yesterday! It's been months since I've relaxed. This time, we'll find your dad at any cost," he exclaimed. Majid trusted Joffrey and knew he was the only person at the company who understood the true purpose of his journey.

When Managing Director Qahtani learned of Majid's plans to return, he too became excited. "Khalli yaji bissur'ah" (May he come quickly), Qahtani exclaimed, repeatedly ordering his favourite Turkish coffee and urging the facilitator to expedite the visa process. The office had been unable to fill the void left by Majid's departure, and they eagerly awaited his return, as expressed by the office secretary, Henna, in her Arabic-accented English.

Within a fortnight, all the preparations for the trip fell into place, but Majid knew he had to present the plan to the family

"Majumon (Majid's pet name), where are you going, leaving all this business behind? Isn't your grandfather too old to manage everything?" questioned his grandmother.

Grandmother's words held truth. Age had started taking its toll on Majid's grandfather, Valyapichi, the man who had built a business empire manufacturing luxury boats. Their construction yards in Beypore were constantly flooded with orders from the Gulf, emirs, sultans, and European business magnates. The company had even expanded overseas. Majid was the sole heir to this vast empire, yet his true intentions remained unknown to everyone. He sought not sustenance but rather a connection to his roots.

Memories of his father were mere fragments from his childhood—a hazy recollection of his father guiding him through the boats under construction, directing the carpenters, and playing games like "camel" together. These heart-warming moments were like precious gems embedded in his mind, painting a picture of a deeply loving person.

As a child, Majid would often sleep next to his mother, feeling her tender embrace. He could recall her caressing him, planting kisses on his cheek, and shedding hot tears that cascaded onto his face.

His mother, Titibees's eyes were always moist, and the burden of her sorrow was etched into his young mind. Majid couldn't help but think her eyes were the most beautiful he had ever seen. Even the eyes of his cousin Minnath and his beloved playmate Leena couldn't compare. Majid fondly remembered the jokes Umma's friends would make during their gatherings in the living room, remarking that her eyes were so deep they could hold the goldfish from his baby aquarium.

Majid never understood why his mother's eyes remained teary, even when surrounded by loved ones. Cook Beepathu would explain that it was because she missed Majid's father. Her cryptic response, promising understanding in due time, left him perplexed.

"What a remarkable person your father was," Beepathu would say. "With his French beard, towering height, and vibrant red face, he commanded attention. Whenever your beautiful mother and your strong, manly father sat together at the threshold of the house, the entire place would illuminate."

"You are a reflection of that towering personality, bearing even the same black mark on your right cheek."

Saying that, she pressed the black mole on his right

cheek and hugged him too. Although his clothes would be stained with dirt, Majid never objected. Beepathu's sweat smelled of the 'pala' flower blooming by the fence. He likes the smell.

Everyone adored Beepathu. She would diligently work while humming folk songs, capturing the hearts of her superiors. Valyummachi, in particular, relied on Beepathu for everything, which fuelled jealousy among the other workers.

"How lucky she is!" exclaimed the other workers in admiration.

Majid was aware that his grandfather, Valyappichi, understood his longing for his father. Did he regret allowing his daughter to marry an Arab? Sometimes, the kindhearted septuagenarian would open up and share his thoughts.

Relatives and locals saw Majid's parents' union as just another Arab marriage. "What's the matter with him, as if there is no other way..." they expressed their surprise.

Valyapicchi, an old English school graduate, perceived his son-in-law as a "Gem of a Gentleman." "We have traveled and sealed deals together. Isn't this the way to understand a man? Your father, Ahmed, was a remarkable young man. None of the marriage proposals we received for your mother were suitable until they fell in love at first sight."

"Tell me, am I wrong?" The grandpa's voice trembled, and Majid couldn't contain his grief.

"Ahmed insisted on delivering a boat to one of his customers himself. Even though he had sailed the seas before, your mother and I disagreed due to security concerns in the Gulf. But his persistence, enthusiasm, and confidence won us over."

"Meanwhile, we received information that an Indian boat had encountered an accident somewhere in the sea near Iran, and everyone on board had survived. However, despite my three trips to Arabia, we never heard from Ahmed. We couldn't even locate his family."

Months and years passed, and the grandpa did everything humanly possible, but Ahmed's fate remained a mystery.

As hope for Ahmed's return began to diminish, marriage proposals for Titibi flooded in, as her charm and pure character were well-known.

"How long will we wait? Consider a divorce and search for a suitable boy," Grandma's words sounded harsh but practical.

A heart-wrenching cry reverberated through the house, igniting a fire within Valyapichi. "Let no one utter another word about it," the grandpa's decree remained upheld to this day.

"I still firmly believe in my heart that he will come back," Valyapichi's unwavering faith granted him self-assurance.

With tearful eyes, Majid's mother pleaded with him to bring his father back. Titibees embraced him tightly and bid him farewell.

"Fee Amanilla (In God's Protection)," Valyapichi also prayed for his safe journey.

The plane prepared for landing, and the captain ensured a smooth arrival. Instructions were given to passengers and crew, and the scheduled landing proceeded. The time lost due to detours could have been made up for by enhanced speed.

Within minutes, the enormous bird gracefully touched down on the ground. The hostess warmly greeted the passengers to the airport, announcing the current time and temperature. As the mercury dropped to a chilly sixteen degrees Celsius, signalling the arrival of winter, it was a relief to have a jacket on.

The plane gradually made its way off the runway and proceeded to taxi towards the terminal, awaiting the aero-bridge. In the distance, at the VIP apron area, people could be spotted eagerly anticipating the arrival of their guests. Their abayas, long cloaks, fluttered in the brisk wind, creating an amusing spectacle.

Upon clearing immigration, Majid stepped out and immediately spotted his chauffeur, Talal, waiting for him.

"Mr. Qahtani was planning to come himself, but unfortunately, he had to stay back as a family guest arrived unexpectedly. He requested that I take you to his home first," Talal informed Majid.

The Mercedes swiftly accelerated towards Qahtani's residence. The road was packed with traffic, despite being a four-lane, two-way street.

"Isn't it Thursday, boss? The start of winter usually brings a rush of people heading out for camping and trips to Bahrain," Talal remarked.

The speedometer needle hovered at one hundred and fifty, yet the velocity wasn't perceptible inside the car. Talal was an adept driver, often compared to the Germans for his skilful control at high speeds.

Many four-wheel drives and trailers were loaded with camping equipment, barbecue stoves, and falcons. When the temperature dropped, the locals here celebrated by venturing out en-masse with their families, seeking suitable locations in the desert. It was as if their ancestral genes, shaped by a nomadic search for oases, compelled them to partake in such excursions.

In the desert, one could find groups of people enjoying themselves in tents, smoking 'hookah', sipping tea and 'gahva' (Arabic coffee), sharing stories, and reciting poetry. Some engaged in falconry and bird hunting with their guns, while children enthusiastically played football. The youngsters, on the other hand, embarked on thrilling desert safaris and indulged in gambling, conquering sand dunes and craters with their four-wheel drive vehicles.

The desert sprawled endlessly, its pale red and golden sands stretching as far as the eye could see. Above, the starry sky bestowed an ethereal beauty upon the desert nights. The evening descended rapidly, casting a light green hue over the surroundings. Only the boundless sky remained constant, resembling a shallow abyss overhead, akin to a queen with sparkling eyes radiating in the blue expanse.

Camping nights are filled with musical intensity. Dancers form a line around the fire, wielding swords, as the Arabian 'dolak', oud, and 'tabla' create a captivating melody. They gracefully dance, raising and lowering their swords, moving their bodies in sync with the rhythm of the song and music. On the ladies' side, a harmonious dance breaks out, following the same captivating rhythm. The scent of burning flesh lingers in the air, emanating from the nearby embers.

"Yakhribbeitak (May your lineage perish)," Talal muttered, lowering his glass as he directed a stream of curses towards another car that had encroached on their lane, dangerously close to colliding with their vehicle. The other driver retaliated with a gesture of their own. Majid patted Talal on the shoulder, offering comfort.

The road became increasingly crowded, causing the cars to slow down. The distance between the bumpers was now mere centimeters. Talal made a decision and veered off the highway, opting for an alternate route. It was an old road with just two lanes, catering to traffic in both directions. The road had a reputation for accidents, as evidenced by the frequent Arabic and English signs that warned, "Beware of crossing camels."

Camels were notorious for their unpredictable movements. They could be seen standing still in herds, only to suddenly sprint across the road with astonishing speed. Talal chuckled at his own remark, saying, "Don't worry, boss. I'll handle it. I doubt we wouldn't make it there if we stuck to the highway."

Majid gazed at the picturesque hues of the evening sun casting its radiant colours upon the rocky hills flanking both sides of the road. These hills, adorned with a multitude of colours, brought back memories of his previous camping trips with friends.

Suddenly, a group of camels emerged from behind a hill and ventured onto the road. A deafening noise was followed by an explosion. In the chaos, Majid was flung out of the car through the door, which had been forced open by the impact. He landed on the back of a camel lying on the ground.

Stunned, Majid clung onto the camel's hump as it swiftly rose and bolted across the desert. The height and speed of the camel made it impossible for him to jump off. Pain coursed through his body, and he sensed bleeding from multiple injuries. He tightened his grip and closed his eyes, gradually slipping into a state of semiconsciousness, overwhelmed by exhaustion and agony.

"Wallahi, haza hafeedee, haza hafeedee, bila shaq" (By God, this is my grandson, this is my grandson, without a doubt)," exclaimed a woman's voice, jolting Majid from his slumber. He realized he was inside a tent, cradled in the lap of a dignified middle-aged woman. The rich scent of oud permeated the air. A nurse diligently tended to his wounds, cleaning and bandaging them.

"Shouf Haza" (Look at this), the woman said, pointing to the mole on Majid's cheek, her gaze directed towards the gathering. Gratitude to God filled the air like a harmonious chorus.

"How did you end up here, Quratul Ain" (my eyeball)?" the woman asked in a raspy voice, showering Majid with kisses. His grandmother was brimming with joy, praising God. It seemed as if her withered breasts had swelled, ready to nurture and provide milk.

Through tear-filled eyes, Majid noticed that some of the men gathered around shared a significant height and had a mole on their right cheek, sporting a "goatee" style beard.

At Times.....

While driving slowly, he endeavoured to soothe his thoughts and align the speedometer needle to a standard level. Hari was enroute to the hospital upon learning that his soulmate, Manu, had been admitted in critical condition to the Medical College Hospital following an accident. However, an inexplicable hesitation subdued him, causing him to question his lack of urgency in rushing to Manu's side. Shouldn't the severity of Manu's condition have spurred distress?

Navigating the speed track with sluggishness, he found himself changing lanes due to incessant honking from behind. The rain-stained sky mirrored nature's discontent, reminiscent of the vulnerability seen in a pregnant woman. He yearned for a heavy downpour, hoping it might cleanse the pollution plaguing his troubled mind.

The memory of Lekha, Manu's wife, painted his thoughts with vivid hues of a distant spring. He pondered whether he had been foolish, relinquishing the sweetness of life for the sake of a societal notion like virginity.

From a young age, his fervour for Lekha had burned brightly. Despite setbacks, she consistently sought his presence, deepening her desire to be close to him.

"Listen, my advice comes from life's lessons. Virginity is but a muscle contraction. Don't waste your life clinging to a myth," offered his spiritual guide, Professor Nandan.

When he confessed to Professor Nandan that his perceived impurity prevented him from making someone as pure as Lekha his life partner, the professor warned, "You will regret this decision. Remember, finding a woman like her is rare in this era."

His preference for admiring flowers from a distance, rather than touching them, struck his friends as peculiar. He had often accompanied Lekha on outings at her insistence. While sharing ice cream on the beach, she once asked, "What holds us back from being together?" Unable to answer that innocent question, he gazed at her face, trying to discern his feelings amidst the vibrant hues of the western horizon.

"I'm ready to sacrifice anything for our relationship. It's important for everyone to know there's no other man in my life," her resolute declaration momentarily startled him.

"Son, Lekha would be a suitable match for you. Why not consider it?" suggested his mother, who had always supported his choices.

"I've found someone even better," he replied. His mother, known for her understanding, remained silent.

Opportunities had a way of consistently beckoning to him. One evening, as he noticed his office secretary Bhavana lingering around with idle hands after the regular office hours, he became attuned to her unspoken intentions. Without reluctance, he decided to initiate a conversation.

"This is entirely new to me, boss. I've never..." Her words, unexpectedly forthcoming, disrupted his train of thought. He gently extricated himself from her embracing arms and made a swift departure. The echo of her voice calling after him transformed into a poignant lament.

Every October full moon, Hari rendezvoused with his friend Amjad in Agra. During their last meeting, Amjad introduced a young girl, saying, "Something you'll appreciate. Brought from Saharanpur, to celebrate the success of the venture you led." Amjad was trying to settle his commitments.

Upon seeing the stunning Jamini Devi, Hari realized Amjad hadn't been exaggerating. As usual, Hari inquired about the girl's circumstances out of curiosity. She revealed her poverty, her father's overwhelming debt, and her fiancé, a watchman who dreamt of her while guarding the cornfields.

She whimpered like a startled fawn. "I'm inexperienced, sir. This is my first time." "Don't worry," he consoled her like a brother.

He withdrew a substantial sum from his suitcase and handed it to her, bidding her farewell. With tearful eyes, the girl knelt at his feet.

"Hanumanji (her god) will protect you, Babu."

Such episodes had occurred multiple times in his life!

He had orchestrated Manu's union with Lekha. Standing at the wedding altar, Hari found it challenging to meet Lekha's gaze.

However, the clock tower of the medical college hospital drew his attention, prompting him to park the car and hurry to the hospital room.

His dear friend Manoj lay there, worn out, wrapped in bandages.

"I'm completely fine now. You're here. I can find peace. I entrust Lekha to you..." His feeble voice trailed off. "No, Manu, no..." Overwhelmed by the tumultuous waves of love and guilt crashing upon his heart, he collapsed beside his friend.

A Doggy Epic

The transition from being a coconut reaper to an insurance officer was an extraordinary tale. In the vast acres of coconut groves owned by Pisharodi, a man named Gopi reigned as a king, making his own decisions and putting them into action. Pisharodi bestowed upon him a great deal of freedom in managing the property and entrusted him completely. Even though the process of harvesting coconuts started at one end of the land at the beginning of the month and took three quarters of the month to complete, neither Gopi nor Pisharodi had any interest in hiring an assistant. Gopi took charge of opening the groves, fertilizing the plants, and ensuring everything was watered properly.

The only visitor to Pisharodi's house was his nephew, Mohanan, who was holding a managerial position at a large insurance company in the city. Mohanan's arrival was a joyous occasion for Gopi. Whenever Mohanan appeared, Gopi would excitedly run towards him, bowing respectfully to receive his orders. The scent of imported perfume and the aroma of cigarettes filled the air, creating a captivating atmosphere for Gopi. As soon as Mohanan noticed him, he would take out a cigarette and offer it to Gopi. In the evenings, Gopi would throw a party to his young boss with homemade toddy and fried chicken, adding to the festive ambiance.

Mohanan admired Gopi's character and recognized his

untapped potential. One day, as Gopi gazed adoringly at Mohanan's car, he asked him,

"Don't you aspire to have something like this?"

Gopi replied, "How could I, Sir? It's just a wishful dream."

Mohanan reassured him, saying, "Your dream will come true, my friend. Let's wait and see."

During their time together, Mohanan discovered many of Gopi's peculiarities, but he didn't feign understanding. He knew that Gopi had successfully fooled Uncle Pisharodi.

Gopi's knack for swiftly counting coconuts while deliberately making mistakes to deceive his uncle was a common occurrence. Mohanan viewed it as cleverness. Furthermore, the fact that Gopi had a circle of beautiful female friends in the village worked in his favour, at least in the eyes of the insurance man.

One evening, while they were enjoying a party, Mohanan asked Gopi, "Would you be interested in coming to the city to work with me?" Gopi replied in surprise, "How is that possible, boss? There aren't many coconut palms in the city."

Mohanan smiled and said to Gopi, locking eyes with him, "I am going to make you a company officer."

Gopi protested, "But I only have a high school education."

Mohanan assured him, "Your resourcefulness in tricking others and your ability to captivate everyone are your strengths."

The following week, the city witnessed a transformed Gopi: clean-shaven, wearing pants, a shirt, and shoes. Mohanan had given him several baths and perfumed him to rid him of the constant scent of coconut and sweat.

Gopi found himself kneeling before the Divisional Manager of the company, who remarked, "I don't require this kind of bowing. Save it for the customers." After a brief explanation about the nature of the job, the Manager added, "All the best, my boy. Work hard, and the sky is the limit for you."

After a few days of training, Gopi emerged as a new man. His joy knew no bounds when he received a business card bearing the name "Gopinathan KP, Development

Officer." Gopi diligently read the Malayalam translation of Dale Carnegie's book, "How to Win Friends...," which had been recommended during the training sessions. It served as his guide and beacon of inspiration.

At first, Gopi embarked on a challenging journey with his superior, Mohanan, hunting for new business opportunities. Armed with a company-provided motorbike, he tirelessly searched for potential customers. However, establishing new business relationships proved to be an arduous task, as the elderly managers in the city had already insured most of the prominent establishments and cultivated strong customer connections.

Gopi couldn't help but agree with a colleague who joined the company with him, acknowledging that "something better can only happen when these cunning old managers are out of the picture." Nevertheless, he remained confident in his abilities. Gopi's first clients were bank managers who had recently relocated to the city. Being newcomers, they had numerous needs, ranging from finding a suitable residence and securing school admissions to obtaining quality meat, fish, and even gas connections. Gopi effortlessly fulfilled all their requirements. Consequently, those who obtained bank loans, such as lorry owners and other businesses, felt obligated to take insurance policies from Gopi due to the insistence of the bank managers.

Within a year, Gopi had become indispensable to all the bank managers. As his business soared from lakhs to crores, the divisional manager called Gopi to offer his congratulations. Additionally, he received a letter from the Area Manager, commending him for exceeding targets within a short period of time.

Through a stroke of luck (don't inquire how), Gopi even managed to acquire the business of Laccadives boat line, catapulting the company's reputation in the city. Gopi became the go-to person not only for insurance matters but also for a wide array of personal and even intimate needs.

His rise was rapid, as the saying goes, happening in leaps and bounds. He surpassed his former chief, Mohanan, and even outshined other tycoons, eventually becoming the manager responsible for most of the incoming business in the company's division.

Gopi now resided in a luxurious villa within a gated community in an upscale area of the city, accompanied by a luxury car. Despite his affluence, a constant sense of inferiority gnawed at him. Though respected within elite circles, he still suspected that people viewed him as a lowly figure. He couldn't help but feel humbled and submissive, despite leading a prosperous life. Moreover, his previous occupation as a coconut reaper had become common knowledge within the community, spread by envious individuals.

It was during this time that Gopi received an invitation from the Pet Lovers Society, requesting a quotation to insure their dogs. The society consisted of affluent ladies and advocates of women's liberation. As Gopi arrived, he was greeted by ladies and young women exuding conceit and grandeur, each cradling a small puppy in their arms. Gopi's eyes gleamed with admiration at their splendour and pride. Soon enough, he became a Casanova among them, sought after for trivial tasks like bathing their dogs and providing them with food. He became a trusted confidant, welcomed in their bedrooms and kitchens. Whenever asked to bend down, he would gracefully drop to his knees. Gopi's mission was to surpass his clients' expectations, a guiding principle of the company.

However, his attention gradually shifted from the ladies to the dogs. Perhaps due to their shared temperament and behaviour, Gopi found himself drawn to the canines. While he possessed some of their traits, he observed their body language and expressions more intently. Nonetheless, the fact that he lacked a wagging tail constantly saddened him.

Gopi's backyard became adorned with kennels of various sizes and shapes. He owned nearly every exotic breed, including Pugs, Labradors, Indian Pariahs, Dalmatians, Pomeranians, and more. Dogs became his pride and joy, and he excelled at dog shows.

Deep down, Gopi harboured a profound disappointment—he had not been born as a dog. He wondered if he had been a dog in a previous life or would become one in the next. In any case, he fervently prayed that he would never be reincarnated as a stray dog.

He often chanted the Tamil proverb, "In the age of forty, a man betrays a dog's character," and tried to live up to it. As he turned forty himself, he pondered whether it was merely a coincidence. The proverb suggested that at this age, a man's behaviour and quirks resemble that of a dog.

One day, Gopi returned home unexpectedly at noon. Upon entering the bedroom, what he witnessed didn't provoke anger but rather curiosity. He noticed movement between his wife's legs, concealed beneath the comforter. When he heard a sound, he realized it was her Pomeranian puppy. His wife lay there with closed eyes, seemingly in a state of blissful forgetfulness. Startled by Gopi's footsteps, the puppy darted out like a captured paramour. Remembering the lesson of viewing everything positively, Gopi chose to ignore it and proceeded to the washroom.

For quite some time, Gopi's wife had been complaining about his snoring, which resembled the growling of an Alsatian, hindering her ability to sleep soundly at night. Whenever Gopi heard a noise, he would rush downstairs and wander around the dark yard, feeling as if he could see without any light. He growled at the cats attempting to enter the compound, chasing them away. He even noticed that his sense of smell had become as strong as a dog's, sniffing every corner of the house and accurately identifying the ingredients in the food items.

One morning, Gopi woke up to his wife's frantic cries. When he tried to ask what was wrong, all that came out was a bark. He didn't find it unusual that his ears had grown long and his body was covered in fur. His hands and feet had transformed into doglike shapes. Jumping off the bed, he stood on all fours, approaching his kneeling wife. She caressed Gopi and made a decision, closing the door behind her before leaving.

Upon her return, she carried a dog collar and carefully dressed Gopi, then guided him into a newly-bought kennel, locking the door from the outside. Gopi hummed softly, expressing either a protest or an expression of love, a sentiment that only his wife could understand.

Sorcery

The background: Mariammachi's gentle fingers meticulously combed through Shirley's shampooed and silky hair, searching for lice. Though they both knew it was a futile exercise, they found solace in these moments of connection. For Shirley, the rhythmic movements of her aunt's fingers provided comfort, while Mariammachi cherished the opportunity to bond with her niece. Their lice-hunting sessions often transformed into insightful discussions, as Mariammachi shared her vast knowledge on various topics.

"Let me tell you about the origins of witchcraft," Mariammachi began, opening a Pandora's Box of information in response to Shirley's curiosity. "According to ancient tales, witchcraft can be traced back to Babylon. It is said that two angels taught people spells to disrupt male-female relationships, but they warned that it was a test from God and should not be used. Unfortunately, the knowledge of witchcraft spread, and people began practicing it despite the warnings." Mariammachi's wisdom transformed her into a walking encyclopedia for Shirley.

"Are there practitioners of witchcraft in our country?" Shirley inquired, her curiosity piqued.

"Witchcraft practitioners exist everywhere, my dear," Mariammachi responded. "I remember our sewing teacher, Parvati, mentioning a scholar who lives on the hilltop bordering our city. Perhaps she sought his assistance at some point. Why do you ask? Is it mere curiosity, or is there something more on your mind?"

Observing Shirley's distressed expression, Mariammachi sensed that something was amiss. As her aunt and confidant, Mariammachi was well aware of the reasons behind Shirley's failed marriage and other personal matters. Shirley had no trouble pouring her heart out to her.

"Be cautious, Shirley. Venturing into this realm can be dangerous," Mariammachi cautioned, her concern evident.

Shirley and Shiraz's relationship went beyond mere friendship; their bond traced back to their childhood and adolescent days. The memories they shared were sweet and cherished. Shirley had never bothered to define the boundaries or limitations of their relationship. One thing she knew for certain was that Shiraz loved her unconditionally, and she reciprocated those feelings equally. However, Shirley grappled with the complexities of male-female relationships.

As the freedom they enjoyed in neighboring households extended into their adulthood, Shirley began to doubt Shiraz's commitment to upholding societal restrictions. Shiraz, in his fervor, tried to convince Shirley of the joys that awaited her in her new marriage, listing the blessings that would come with it.

Confusion and grief overwhelmed Shirley. She questioned whether Shiraz, despite excelling in academics and business, truly understood anything at all. Was he merely fooling himself or lacking the courage to break free from society's rules?

In her heart, Shirley knew there was no room for another man. She knew nothing else.

On the screen: One evening, as Shirley and Parvathi teacher approached the outskirts of the city, the setting sun cast a golden glow. Climbing the steep hill that would lead them to the monastery of the "Holistic Healer" Pavaran would take around twenty minutes. Struggling to maintain her composure, Shirley recalled the saying, "The goal validates the path."

Throughout their journey, Parvati sang Pavaran's praises, recounting numerous miracles attributed to him, such as reuniting lovers and resolving marital problems.

Along the way, they passed signs in Malayalam, Kannada, Tamil, and English, all pointing towards the ashram. "Well, at least the ashram seems to transcend state boundaries, if not international ones," Shirley playfully teased her teacher. However, her jest didn't amuse Parvati, who replied, "Don't trivialize it, dear. The ashram holds great significance."

Did her heart quicken as she approached the ashram? She tightly held her teacher's hand. Was it not a guilty conscience troubling her more than meeting the healer? If something happened to Shiraz... Was she diving into a pool of trouble? No, this was her life, and she had no second thoughts. Shirley consoled herself.

"Baby, don't worry. Pavaran is a good man," how could her teacher, a tailoring trainer, immersed in the world of sewing threads, understand the enigma within her.

When they reached the plain, a polished black building stood before them. Glowing letters beneath the ashram's huge signboard read, "Holistic Healer Dr. Pavaran," accompanied by a dozen or so degrees.

Upon entering the ashram, as they removed their footwear, Shirley felt a sensation as if her feet were being washed by flowing water. An attendant dressed in Mughal style bowed slightly and waved them inside.

"It's not your turn yet, but you can wait comfortably in the waiting room. There's tea and snacks available if you'd like," the attendant informed them.

A long, wide corridor with a red carpet stretched ahead, lined with life-like images of gods and malevolent spirits on both sides. Bhadrakali, the impaled goddess of horror, a distorted image of Lucifer, demons, genies of various names, sumo fighters, tigers and lions hunting other animals -- all backlit to intensify the fright. Stuffed buffalo, fox, and eagle heads adorned the walls, adding to the eerie atmosphere. Bats and sparrows fluttered in the hall, while massive dogs of exotic breeds roamed around. Shirley felt like she had stepped onto the set of a horror film. The healer appeared as a cunning figure, poised to deceive unsuspecting people.

While Parvati teacher enjoyed vada and tea, Shirley had no appetite. Through the glass wall of the waiting room, she could see another room where people dressed in purple, wearing turbans and long robes, with their hair tied above their heads, sat in a circle and chanted some kind of mantra.

Finally, their token number appeared on the electronic board. Shirley followed the teacher who covered her head gracefully as she entered, with the edge of her sari.

A faint smoky scent hung in the air, accompanied by an unfamiliar fragrance. Dr. Pavaran's chamber was adorned with Persian carpets and Italian sofas, softly illuminated by dim candlelight. Seated on a thronelike chair was a portly figure whose face reminded Shirley of a chimpanzee. He gestured for them to sit on a low bench before him.

"You look beautiful. The one who abandoned you is a fool," Pavaran said without preamble. He proceeded to list all of Shirley's problems and past life as if he were a fortune-teller. Shirley now suspected that Parvati teacher must have informed him of everything in advance. Unable to meet Shirley's stern gaze, the teacher lowered her head.

"Let's fix this. But everything must remain confidential," Pavaran delved into the matter, explaining in detail what needed to be done—burial of plaques, wearing of amulets, performing sacrifices, applying frog remedies, and more.

"Don't worry, I will take care of everything myself," the teacher assured Shirley, who hesitated. But it was Pavaran's lewd body language, winks, and laughter that disturbed her the most.

They returned after purchasing the necessary items and paying a hefty fee.

Days passed uneventfully. In the meantime, the teacher diligently followed the magician's instructions. Shirley grew frustrated with the knots and cords, often feeling the urge to discard them.

They attended two more sessions with Pavaran. On the third visit, Mariammachi joined them, uneasy and concerned about her niece's pitiful state. Mariammachi posed questions to Pavaran, inquiring about the effectiveness of his practices.

"...Refunds and such are not a problem. Just wait until the next black moon, and it will be done," Pavaran answered, leaving Mariammachi feeling unsettled. They left with a note for the eclipse preparations and a fairly large packet.

"I don't trust his lethargy. Perhaps he's a fraudster. Nonetheless, I will ensure your safety," Mariammachi vowed.

Only a few days remained until the black moon. Shirley began her preparations. "What an intriguing affair!" Mariammachi marvelled. Pavaran's note was read repeatedly, and the packet he provided contained everything—the incense burner, pieces of wood resembling oud, and aromatic ointments for application on the body.

On the appointed day, Shirley woke up early, eager for the dawn of her new life. The entire house was meticulously cleaned, with special attention given to the bedroom. By evening, she could hardly sit still. The reluctant housemaid was sent away, granted two days' leave. She paced around the house, unable to bear the frenzy that consumed her.

Meanwhile, she found solace in conversing with birds, flowers, and trees. "Today, my beloved is coming," she murmured, her excitement evident. She longed to express her joy through song and dance.

As dusk began to settle, there was still much to be done. She made her way to the bedroom, carefully spreading a fresh bed sheet and adorning it with jasmine flowers. Fruits and flowers were thoughtfully arranged on the side table, and she ensured that the flask contained the milk she had prepared earlier.

The stage was set, but now she had to prepare herself. Selecting her most exquisite transparent nightgown, she indulged in a meticulous bath. After drying her body, she shed the robe she had been wearing and positioned herself on a cane chair, her naked form exposed to the fragrant incense emanating from the steaming censor beneath. "Let the perfume's smoke touch every part of your body," Pavaran had advised. She proceeded to apply ointment while gazing at her reflection in the mirror. The sight of her toned body, with big eyes resembling a tranquil pool of water, balanced lips, and cherubic cheeks, affirmed Pavaran's assertion—her beauty was captivating.

Shirley dressed in her night clothes, enjoyed a light meal with a hum. Now, she could only wait. "If you hear the song of the midnight bird calling its mate, you can be sure that he has arrived," Pavaran had written.

Suddenly, a gentle knock at the back door startled her. Peering through the window, she spotted Mariammachi. "This Ammachi," she thought irritably. Observing Shirley's appearance, Mariammachi burst into laughter before tenderly kissing her forehead, tears welling in her eyes.

"I couldn't sleep because of you, dear. Don't worry, I won't disturb you. I'll lie down on the corner bed," Ammachi reassured, then retired to her room downstairs.

Would this wait be endless? Shirley, awaiting the song of the midnight bird, eventually succumbed to slumber.

"Seeru, where have you been all this time?" she softly uttered

"I was searching for you, Sherry," came the reply.

"We haven't forgotten our old pet names, have we?" she said, nestling into Shiraz's open embrace, finding solace in the safety of his strong arms.

"Your body odour drives me crazy," he confessed.

"Seeru, take your time. The night is still young. I want to talk to you a lot. I have kept everything precious unsullied for you."

"I know, Sherry. I trust you."

Their words faded away, and she felt as if she were fluttering in the gentle breeze. Where was this wind taking her? It seemed that in the distance, notes and tones harmoniously converged to create a melodious music.

"Are you listening to the music of the rain? The wet land, the thirsty land.

Rain, rain again. Even the creepers thrive."

"I can't... I can't..." she trailed off………..

The sound of the doorbell echoed through the house, followed by the shattering of objects and commotion from downstairs. Shirley, startled awake, hurried down, bewildered by the scene before her. Mariammachi stood there, a victorious smile adorning her face as she clutched something heavy in her hands, panting heavily. Pavaran lay on the floor, moaning and groaning amidst a pool of blood.

In that moment, Shirley's feelings shifted from contempt for Pavaran to a surge of gratitude, while disdain for Mariammachi took hold.

A Millennium Spectacle

The year 2000 was marked by a terrifying event in the history of the world. As the transition from the 1900s to the new millennium approached, around the turn of the 20th century, fears arose regarding potential problems arising from the change in year format in calendars and storage of calendar details in computer systems. This unprecedented level of fear was primarily due to the anticipated disruptions to computer systems and programs that had to distinguish between the years 1900 and 2000. People, especially in Western countries, started stockpiling essential supplies, purchasing generators, withdrawing money from banks to prepare for a catastrophic event that might occur as they ushered in the new century.

Financial institutions, particularly banks, were hit the hardest by this situation. Consumers began withdrawing money en masse, causing a significant strain on banks' resources. Even though banks were willing to provide loans to help maintain liquidity and tackle the crisis, people were reluctant to buy properties or make long term investments. As a result, the banking sector faced severe difficulties. In response to this situation and to exploit it, Western computer companies took action. Billions of dollars were spent by banks and other financial corporations to make the necessary changes. Gulf banks were not exempt from this phenomenon; they had to alter their systems and policies to comply with global standards. However, Gulf banks emerged as the most profitable due to their proactive approach in catering to the needs of individuals who adhere to Islamic principles. While the Gulf banks did face the same Y2K-related challenges, they managed to modernize their computer programs and systems by collaborating with experts and complying with regulations.

However, as the Y2K system upgrade was carried out, a realization dawned that the problem wasn't as dire as anticipated. Only a few disruptions occurred in computer systems, and the panic that had gripped consumers seemed unnecessary. The heightened concerns about the potential consequences of Y2K vanished, leaving a valuable lesson for both businesses and consumers alike. The experience served as a reminder that being informed and seeking expert advice were crucial in such situations.

But the system upgrade does not suffice, it stands ahead with the banner of making consumers aware, a task that has gained significance along with the technological advancements in service offered by experts.

It was during this period that I was working as a Corporate Marketing Communication Manager in one of the major banks in the Gulf. I was responsible for handling all responses to the sentiments of customers and users, as well as the perceptions of all advertising materials of the bank. In the context of the Y2K issue, I myself hold the responsibility to gain their confidence through their emotions and to formulate the responsible response - even though its technical aspect is managed by the experts in the area.

My bank had enlisted the services of Stuart Arnold, a charismatic young man from Britain, and his team to implement necessary changes, including computer programs and accounting systems, to ensure Y2K compliance. Stuart consistently organized meetings between his team and my Communications team, fostering collaborative progress in both areas.

The bank's Chief Executive Officer (CEO) frequently

reached out to me, seeking updates on the ongoing work, reflecting his evident concern. It fell upon him to apprise the Board of Directors of the actual state of affairs. As time passed, comprehending the gravity of the situation, the CEO's anxiety became contagious, affecting me as well. An unspoken "emergency" atmosphere permeated my office operations. I challenged the PR and advertising agencies involved in the project, pushing them to their limits. Leaves for the staff were temporarily suspended during this period.

"Fret not, Mohammad. We're set to secure the Chairman's approval," Stuart reassured me. With September looming, a mere three months remained until the pivotal day. I orchestrated advertisements across major media platforms, incurring costs amounting to millions of riyals, spanning print and television commercials. The allocations for newspaper and television advertising competed within the budgetary constraints. During that period, the utilization of social media was not as extensive as it is now.

Both teams stood prepared. Management had greenlit my conceptual plans alongside Stuart's technical strategies. The time had come to meticulously present everything to the Chairman and the Board of Directors, seeking their endorsement. In a meeting where both the Board of Directors and management were present, our task was to articulate each step with logic and precision.

Finally, the long-awaited day dawned. The bank's central conference hall had been meticulously prepared to host the upcoming event. The facility management team from my department initiated the final arrangements. They diligently inspected and verified the functionality of the sound systems, projectors, and laptops. Like two unified armies converging on the battlefield, poised to confront a shared enigmatic adversary, both teams honed their respective resources. Amidst a backdrop of determined smiles, Stuart could be observed earnestly imparting last-minute instructions to his team, striving for a flawless presentation.

Gradually, attendees began to arrive. Vice Presidents and managers, rallying under the CEO's guidance, graced the scene first, followed by directors and esteemed board members. All that remained was the chairman's presence. With a successful microphone test confirming its operational prowess, the sound technician handed over a discreet pocket mike to Stuart.

At last, the chairman made his entrance. In a gesture reminiscent of Arabic tradition, the entire assembly rose, offering their salutations. As the chairman assumed his seat, a subtle nod from the CEO directed me to initiate the proceedings. With a warm welcome, I acquainted the audience with the presentation's content and the proposed agenda. My talk also conveyed a reassuring message to everyone and detailed the essence.

Concluding my address, I invited Stuart to approach the podium and commence his presentation. However, to my dismay, he was conspicuously absent, nowhere to be found. I scanned the surroundings, recalling that I had sighted him prior to the chairman's arrival. Astonishingly, his team members were equally oblivious to his whereabouts. Panic surged within me, causing perspiration despite the coolness of the air-conditioned hall. The audience mirrored the unease, voicing their discontent through audible disturbances.

In this pivotal juncture, where could he have vanished? My mind raced as I hastened towards the adjacent in-house library, suspecting he might have sought a lastminute reference there. Regrettably, my search proved fruitless. Could he have slipped away for a coffee or a swift snack at Suleiman's cafeteria, enticed by his beloved 'Porotta Dip'*?

Taking swift action, I dispatched our reliable driver, Sukumaran, on a mission to scour every conceivable location for Stuart, instructing him to promptly update me upon discovery.

Through subtle yet pointed gestures, the CEO inadvertently conveyed his growing impatience with the delayed start of the presentation. The stakes were high, with the risk of tarnishing his reputation in front of the Chairman and the esteemed board. Any further delay could lead to the Chairman's departure, potentially upending the entire situation. As my concerns escalated, my imagination took a more fantastical turn. Could this Y2K problem have metamorphosed into an apparition, haunting Stuart and steering him off course?

Amidst this uncertainty, Hasan Nour, Stuart's Bengali assistant, stepped into the spotlight, seemingly prepared to take over the presentation. While Hasan was undoubtedly proficient in his role, my reservations regarding his English-speaking clarity prevented me from allowing this transition to occur.

Abruptly, a thunderous clap-like sound reverberated through the hall, leaving everyone in a state of bewilderment, followed by an immediate hush that settled over the audience like a heavy fog. Then, another sound arose—a delicate, rhythmic pattern akin to water droplets falling from a child's umbrella during the monsoon season, creating a steady, tranquil melody. This peculiar sound persisted for a minute, gradually growing in intensity until it transformed into an echoing resonance reminiscent of an elephant's triumphant trumpet. The unexpectedness of this noise induced panic, causing heads to swivel in search of its origin. The impending occurrence seemed unprecedented, shrouded in mystery.

Subsequently, a new sound emerged, peculiar yet relentless—akin to water flowing from a previously obstructed faucet, releasing in an unbroken stream. Accompanying it was a rhythmic, potent thumping resembling the determined beat of a mallet upon wood. The resounding 'Thapp Thapp' echoed, mimicking the robust cadence of purposeful boot steps. Was this the pivotal moment when the perplexing Y2K predicament that had plagued us was on the brink of resolution? An eerie hush reclaimed the atmosphere, thick with anticipation.

Then... the tension-laden air gave way to that sound, which reverberated throughout the hall. In response, nods of realization and grins of relief swept through the audience, while a sudden eruption of laughter burst forth from the hallways.

Emerging from the washroom, Stuart appeared, a foolish yet triumphant smile gracing his face. His strides were brimming with confidence, each step resonating like a march of determination. Onstage, we held our breath in harmony with the rhythm. A quick check of Stuart's microphone confirmed its operational state—still switched on and fully functional within his pocket.

Once again, the atmosphere was punctuated by the contagious sound of laughter, akin to the jubilant explosion of bursting fireworks. This was the audible manifestation of the 'Y2K problem' finally being cracked. Its resonance lingered, cascading like an unblocked stream, as if a weighty burden had been lifted. Moments seemed suspended in time.

With an air of triumph, the resonant sound danced in the air, uniting the entire sky in a chorus of mirth. Laughter and applause resonated throughout the hall, filling it with a vibrant energy. Heads tilted back in unrestrained amusement, as a procession of joy spread from the washroom to the main hall. Faces held high, laughter flowed freely, a testament to overcoming the formidable struggle. The presentation, at long last, drew to a close. Amidst applause and commendations from the board members, a sense of accomplishment permeated the air, marking the successful conclusion of our journey.

*Porrotta:*A Kerala dish*

"Breach of Purity"

Kashif, the newlywed groom, was engrossed in prayer as Dilshad quietly entered the room carrying a tray laden with milk and an assortment of fruits. Her steps were accompanied by a hint of shyness, but she exhibited no trace of hesitation. As she pondered the purpose of his prayer, he concluded his devotions and settled on the edge of the bed. The beige-coloured sherwani he wore accentuated his handsomeness.

Attempting to divert Kashif's gaze away from the floor, Dilshad's efforts proved futile. Despite the chill from the air conditioner, she was drenched in sweat beneath the weighty drapery of her specially ordered saree and the intricate jewellery adorning her. Umma's(mother) strict decree had bound her to wearing this attire until Kashif had witnessed it all; only then could she change into more comfortable clothing.

Perplexed about the norms of such occasions, she gingerly picked up the glass of milk and seated herself beside him on the bed. A delusion took hold of Dilshad, envisioning her saree being unravelled, liberating her from the burden of pearl necklaces and heavy diamond chains. Almost as if her wish had been communicated to them, the bangles on her arms, adorned with peacock motifs, emitted a soft tinkling sound and seemed to shimmer with a playful gleam. Edging closer to Kashif, she made an attempt to clasp his hand.

However, Kashif's words, uttered in his native dialect and revealing his lineage, land, and clan, struck a discordant note within her. "Refrain from touching me, for my ablution* will be nullified," he pronounced.

Dilshad, who valued authenticity above all else, felt not only displeasure but also a sense of repugnance. She would have, under different circumstances, laughed and dismissed the sentiment. She had not anticipated this. When news of her impending marriage to Kashif spread, her friends' collective reaction was, "Are you out of your mind?"

Among their college peers, Kashif stood out due to his academic prowess and devotion, which had earned him the moniker "Vegetable." Nevertheless, it seemed that many secretly yearned for the attention of this handsome introvert. Inadvertantly, Dilshad harboured her own longing for him. As marriage proposals flooded in, her father insisted on finding a groom who was both educated and religiously conscientious. And so, during their search, Kashif emerged as a prospect. Initially, Dilshad was enthralled. Yet, as she apprehensively faced the prospect of her first night, a nagging fear arose – could Kashif indeed live up to the persona he had adopted during his college days? Did the echoes of her classmates' laughter reverberate within the walls of her bridal chamber?.........

Years down the line, Dilshad fondly reflects on the breach of purity that unfolded that very night, finding it both sweet and precious. It was a moment when Kashif's ablution was unexpectedly interrupted. From her current vantage point of contentment, having become a mother to five children, preserving the B Tech degree she has earned as a frozen keepsake, she holds onto the memory dearly.

(Ablution: A ceremonial act of washing the face and limbs in preparation for Muslim prayer, which would be invalidated, as some believe, by a touch of opposite gender)